To M...

PSYCHIC DETECTIVE

by Nancy O. Weber
with
Iris Nevins

Nancy O Weber

Published By The Unlimited Mind Publications

First Edition

Published by The Unlimited Mind Publications
(A subsidiary of N.O.W. Inc.)
P.O.Box 1132
Denville NJ 07834

Printed and bound by
PK Graphics
75 Varick Street
New York City, NY 10013

ISBN-0-9646118-0-5

Dedication

I would like to first thank Iris Nevins, for without her belief in my work and her untiring willingness to keep me on track, I would never have completed this work. Iris' tasks were to interview the police and all other parties, extract their statements and weave them into my recollections.

When I consider what it has taken to recover from being a crime victim, I don't know who to thank first for my ability to stand strong and loving in this sometimes brutal world. For all the love shared through all of my life, I thank each and every sentient being. I wish to thank my husband Dick, who's dedication to loving and believing in me has helped empower my life, and to everyone at the International Women's Writing Guild, especially Hannalore Hahn, Tatiana Stoumen and Alice Orr.

To the law enforcement officers who never lose their focus on what is needed and remain caring despite what they witness, thank you. If not for their concern I would never have had the opportunity to further my own healing and help those I truly believe I can help.

Heartfelt thanks to Paul Katz for his friendship and creative genius.

To Tom Walker for his support and belief in my work.

To my children, Rebecca and Jesse and all children. May our work help towards making your journey a safe one.

᪥᪥᪥᪥᪥᪥᪥᪥᪥᪥᪥᪥

Where permission has been granted, a person's full name has been used. Those people who have not given permission or for the sake of their privacy, have been given false names and only given a first name.

In writing my story, I decided that it would be wise to have Iris interview those police officers and family members that I worked with. I wrote the stories, Iris wrote the appendix and some of the animal chapters that were actually originally interviews.

Contents

PROLOGUE
NANCY'S DREAM:

1975 - It startled me to see this man approach. I couldn't make out his face. It was almost completely covered with a black hood that draped down into a floor length cape. He reached out with both hands and gave me a large chunk of gold. Its shape suggested it had been melted down from a sculpting. He then thrust his arm out and pointed to a sign on a city street. The sign read "Wise Publishing". "But I don't write," was my only thought. Startled by the thought, I jumped out of my dream and sat awake looking at the night sky.

1977 - Psychic reader Margaret Twedell Flavell was in from England and I was having my yearly check-up. "A woman will offer to write a book with you, and you will do it."

"Margaret, I don't write, and to tell you the truth, I don't even desire to write. Maybe some poetry, but not a book."

Margaret's only answer was the twinkle in her eyes. Wherever you are, dear lady, I thank you for all your advice, wisdom and counsel, but most of all I thank you for your love.

IRIS' DREAM:

I am a paper marblizer by trade. A book was handed to me in a very vivid dream by a fellow marbler, Christopher Weimann, who had died the previous year. The book was published as a limited edition by a small press in Pennsylvania in 1990.

Friends and I would occasionally joke about my going to sleep and dreaming up another book, but I considered it a once in a lifetime oddity. This was not to be the case, however.

I always assumed that if I did have any more books handed to me in dreams, they would be concerning the topic of marbling. I woke with amazement early in the morning of March 21, 1992, when I was handed yet another book in a dream. My amazement was not so much at the fact that it was happening again, but rather that the book had nothing to do with paper marbling. It was a paperback titled, *A Different Way Of Seeing*, and subtitled *The Life of Psychic, Nancy Weber*. Upon further inspection I saw that the book had been written by Nancy and myself together.

When I told Nancy about this "dream book" she said, "Finally I know who the other woman is."

Psychic detects criminals with her 'inner eye'

By JULIE BEGLIN

When Nancy Fuchs was appointed a special officer with the Mt. Olive Police Department in 1981, it wasn't for the usual reasons of helping with crowd control or other volunteer activities.

She helped the department, not with her eyes or ears or strength but with what some people call an inner eye. Fuchs, who is now married and uses the name Nancy Fuchs Weber, worked on criminal cases as a psychic.

Always conscious of her unusual abilities, Fuchs Weber, who now lives in Denville, said she didn't think to put the powers to use in criminal investigation until 1979, when it was suggested to her by a policewoman whose then-4-year-old son she was teaching karate to her then-4-year-old son.

The policewoman had read a local newspaper article about Fuchs Weber helping neighbors find lost pets and asked if she could help on a recent criminal case.

"I said, 'You have to tell me the kind of case it is, nothing else,'" Fuchs Weber recalled. The instructor said it was rape, and Fuchs Weber said she immediately had a vision "of a man hitting a female with a rock on the head." She said she described the man physically and what he was like emotionally.

The following week, Detective Ross English came to the karate class to talk to Fuchs Weber, she said. When he suggested that her vision was not of the right man, Fuchs Weber got up and walked across the floor with a limp. "No, he walks like this," she recalled telling English. She added, "I become whoever it is for a moment."

Soon afterward, Fuchs Weber was asked to work on the case with the Mt. Olive police. The rapist was later caught, indicted and convicted.

In 1981, she was awarded a plaque by Morris County Sheriff John Fox for helping in the return of three missing children.

Detective Sgt. Ed Katona, who has been on the Mt. Olive force for 10 years, said that Fuchs Weber was used on a couple of homicide cases and a still unresolved 1976 case in which unidentified skeletal remains were found off Route 80.

"She provides information, and many times we have discovered that same information true as the investigation proceeds," he said. "All the information may not pertain, but at some point, it's uncanny."

He added, however, that use of her or any psychic is very uncommon.

"This is not an accepted practice and is not discussed on any active cases that we are involved in now," he stressed.

Psychic Nancy Fuchs Weber of Denville received the gratitude of Morris County for her help in locating missing children.

Adding that none of a psychic's information can be used to get a search warrant or to establish probable cause, he said, "The case has got to be a case where you have absolutely nothing — (where) you have a choice to go no-where or to take a shot in the dark and see what light these people can shed on it —"

These days, Fuchs Weber rarely works on criminal investigations, partly because she was tired of dealing with skepticism from public and political organizations and partly because her husband, whom she married in February 1985, asked her to stop.

She keeps a full schedule lecturing, counseling and teaching about the powers of the mind, as well as writing fiction and non-fiction about her criminal case work.

Fuchs Weber said she started working with law enforcement because she believes that people must take a stand and help each other.

A victim of several violent crimes herself—including molestation, at age 12, by a teacher into whose class she was sent back—Fuchs Weber said she vowed at a young age never to put another person in an unsafe situation.

Through this philosophy, as well as discovering that her previous work as a nurse didn't fully heal "mind-body-spirit" ailments, as she put it, Fuchs Weber began to use her psychic abilities for career and volunteer work.

"I believe that the mind's energy is everywhere, all the time," she said, "and I've had enough proof."

When she was growing up, she was taunted by other children as a witch because, she said, "I would tell them things that were going to happen, and I would be 100 percent accurate."

The response, she said, "made me feel very uncomfortable with what I've come to learn is a gift."

After moving to Mt. Olive from New York, Fuchs Weber gradually let her abilities become known by telling neighbors where their missing pets were and what time they would return home.

She also helped solve a robbery of her own home.

In 1983, Fuchs Weber said, she was having lunch with a friend. Suddenly, she got down her fork and said, "I'm being robbed."

She returned to the house to find it had been robbed, as she expected. She said she told the police "where the evidence would be, where they had taken it." She also brought in a brass lamp to be fingerprinted once she realized the burglars didn't wear gloves.

"It took eight hours from the actual incident to a full confession," she said.

Criminal trial attorney John M. Iaciofano, who knows Fuchs Weber personally and has defended cases in which psychics have played some role in the investigation, said, "Nancy is a very, very interesting, very bright, very nice person.

"I think as a member of the somewhat skeptical — non-psychic population, people like us always tend to look a little crossed-eyed at first at people whose abilities are different than ours."

He added that although psychics "obviously have been used by just about every law-enforcement agency that there is, they classically are used in intermediary stages and on a side to discover evidence that was undiscoverable or un-locatable or unknown."

Fuchs Weber said that even though her ability is seen by some people as a farce involving "turban-wearing sorts," when she lectures at schools, discusses her work with her two children's friends and meets many professionals, the reaction is different.

"I find that most of society that I run into has tremendous respect for my work once they know what I do," she said.

If she were asked to work on another criminal investigation, she would first ask her husband, she laughed, adding that if the case moved her, she would feel obliged to help any way she could.

CHAPTER ONE
<u>WHERE ARE MY CHILDREN?</u>

"Hi, Nancy, this is Glen from WMTR. We just got a call from a woman who said her grandchildren were abducted and she wanted your number. Can we give it to her?"

I had just returned home from a radio talk show about my psychic gifts when the producer called.

"Absolutely. Tell her I'll be waiting." I quickly prepared a cup of tea and wondered what I would be dealing with. The phone rang within 5 minutes.

"Hello, I'm Mrs. Keyes. I heard you a little while ago and I thought maybe you could help my daughter. Her children were stolen by her ex-husband and she has no idea where they are."

"I don't know what I can do. All I can do is attempt to help, I really don't know what I will be capable of. Each case I work on and every situation is so different. Why don't you have your daughter call me. Does she live in New Jersey?"

"Yes".

"Do you think she can come to my office in my home? I think it would be easier for us in person."

"Can she call you tonight?"

"Sure, just tell her I finish work at about 8:00 PM tonight. Anytime after that and before 10."

We rang off and years of discipline went kicking in. Every day I thank the teachers of Brooklyn College Nursing and my early years of training. They keep paying off. I didn't want to second guess the events I was about to get involved in so I moved my mind and body into a routine of work.

8:30PM..."Hello, my mother called you today. I'm Jillian."

"Oh, yes, hi Jillian. Your mother told me your children were taken by your ex-husband. Please don't fill me in right now. There will be plenty of time to tell me what you know after I look into it my way. Do you have photos of your children and can you come to my home office in Budd Lake?"

"Yes, I can and I'll bring the photos. Anything else I need to bring?"

"Just an open mind. I really don't think I need anything else to start with. You know I can't promise you results."

"I know, could I bring someone from the Sheriffs' office? He's an investigator who is helping me."

"Of course, bring anyone you want. I'll have a tape recorder going and you will keep the tape we make. Sometimes things come to me in pieces like a jigsaw puzzle and we have to figure it out afterwards. I never know beforehand how things will go."

"How much do you charge?"

"Jillian, by the time it's over you will be deep in debt from your search. I'm not about to add to your burdens. There will be no charge for any of my services. Feel free to use me and call on me as needed."

We hung up, and my mind tried to go numb but my heart wouldn't let it.

How could I charge her? I could be next. What if my own ex-husband, Gil wins his custody suit? What if he doesn't? He'd tried to snatch my daughter just to hurt me. He cares as little for her welfare as Jillian's ex cares for his children.

The next few days I was afraid to let my children out of my sight. Normally they could run around in the mall, visit friends and in general had a lot of freedom. These days were different. The fear was so strong I could hear the beat of my heart day and night. My eyes were commanded to stay frozen on my children. Don't let them out of sight for a second. That is all it takes. I was running on empty, exhausted and terrified.

The month we moved to New Jersey Gil served me with papers, a custody suit in which he made horrendous accusations. Unfortunately I wasn't wise enough then to recognize his projections. Had I known, he'd be dead and I would probably be writing this from jail.

Five evenings after the call, Jillian arrived with Investigator Lou Masterbone. The sweetest face had the saddest smile. Her dimples couldn't hide, even from the pain. Her eyes were in a constant state of terror, large pale blue freaked out eyes. The man standing next to her had eyes and hair as dark as hers were light. His black mustache accentuated his Mediterranean heritage.

We went upstairs to my office. Jillian and I sat on my old brown plaid couch and Lou sat opposite us in a pale blue overstuffed chair. Old, comfortable furniture in a room that was painted a soft blue to encourage peaceful feelings. It felt good to be able to focus on an issue, one that I might be able to help move. Lou immediately jumped in:

"I don't believe in any of this, but if you can help Jillian, I'll listen."

"I brought the photo you asked for. It's not very good, but all three children are in it", Jillian said.

"Let me see it, please."

Just then my dog, Ramona walked in and promptly lay down on my feet. She was very devoted to her rest, and she needed a mommy all the time. Her brown long hair was soft to my touch.

Her tail curled happily as she closed her eyes in contentment.

The photo slowly came alive. A man was standing to the left of a pony with his back to me. A little girl was on the pony and on the right was another little girl and a very little boy.

"That's your ex with the children. He was violent with you, wasn't he?"

I could hear Jillian's sharp intake of breath:

"Yes, he was, that's why I divorced him."

"Don't worry, he won't hurt the children, he's more careless than violent now. He doesn't hate them, he hates you. He believed he should have the children, and when the courts said no, he had a back up plan. You haven't seen or heard from them for several months. Is that true?"

"Not for 10 months. The day he lost the appeal to have the children, he had them for a visit and I never saw them again."

"He has a friend who owns a truck, he was packed and waiting, expecting the worst. Then went directly across country. There was a woman who also helped. She watched the children when he settled in a new state. Texas, he went to Texas. I've got to get a map. I'll be right back."

I rushed to my sons' bedroom and pulled out our Americana Encyclopedia, section T.

"Got it," as I settled back on the couch. Ramona resettled back on my feet, having hardly moved.

"Here, here he is, Uliss, Texas. I could feel them there."

Lou's eyes were big, "Yeah, we know he went there, Some detective located him there for a while, but he must have known, he moved and we lost him."

Jillian told me that her former husband, Joe had been living in the family home with their three children, Diane, seven, Jean, six, and John, three. They had a custody trial in June of 1980 in which Jillian was awarded custody of the children and the house. The judge granted Joe one more week with the children, after which he was to vacate and she would move back in with them. After six days Joe disappeared with the children and Jillian did not see them for the next thirteen months.

Jillian was very worried. Joe never adequately cared for the children. Diane was required to be the mother. She had to do all the cooking and cleaning and watch over the two younger children. He had originally been granted custody two years earlier when they were divorced. She found out later that she had lost because her first attorney never requested that she be put back in the house with the children. Jillian was told that the judge said that the status quo was to remain.

Jillian: Originally, I moved out of the house without the children because Joe left me for two weeks. Then he suddenly returned and announced that he was not leaving no matter what. Three days later I left because I was afraid of him. He had already put me in the hospital with a severe beating. I went to my lawyer and said I could not go back there. This is how the mix up occurred, allowing Joe to get custody. When I saw he was not caring for the children well I went back to court to try to get them.

I had managed to find Joe and the children once. The police had traced him to Texas. Just by coincidence they were going to another call in his apartment complex. They noticed he had New Jersey license plates and looked up the number. They found there was a warrant for his arrest."

Nancy: Why was there a warrant for his arrest?

Jillian: Because legally he was not the custodial parent and he had taken the kids across state lines.

Nancy: Is it a crime or misdemeanor ?

Jillian: It's a misdemeanor. Though they had found him they could virtually do nothing. They would not take the children. The police went to his apartment, knocked on the door and told him they had a warrant for his arrest. They told him not to leave, and of course he left. I flew to Texas that night with only the clothes on my back. I thought I would finally have them back, but when I arrived, they had gone. We did not know where.

I think Joe had time to leave because I could not simply go and get the children. I was forced to go through legal channels. I had to first spend a lot of time at the police station. First my attorney in New Jersey got me a Texas attorney I had to see. Then we had to go to court that day so the state of Texas could award me custody of my children. When I finally got to his apartment it was empty. They were gone.

I spent the next five days in Texas trying to trace Joe. He had once worked for a printing company that had a Dallas office. He used them for an employment reference to get his apartment. I tried to see if they knew anything about where he could have gone. I tried contacting the rental agency, but still no luck. The apartment was beautiful, so he must have had money. Later I found out his mother had been sending him money.

(See appendix A for further recountings of Jillian on this case, and her own creative attempts to re-unite with her children)

Looking at the map of the United States my eyes shifted to California.

"He's in California now".

"Where in California?" Lou wanted to know.

Two hours had passed since we first sat down.

"Southern half, near the coast. He has a job there. The children are okay. One of your daughters has had stitches on her upper lip."

"What did he do?"

"He didn't do it, Jillian. A dog jumped up and bit her. He took her to the emergency room and they stitched it. She's fine and not afraid of dogs."

"Do they ask about me?"

"Sure they do. He told them mommy is sick and can't be with them now."

"Will I ever see them again?"

"Absolutely..."

"Where in Southern California?" Lou persisted.

" 'E' street, I see the street sign."

"I need a town, can you give me the name of the town.?"

Just them my dog looked up and nudged me with her nose.

"Ramona," I called out to her.

"Ramona, California?" Lou Asked

Why not?

"Yes, Ramona, California."

"How can we check it out without him leaving?" Lou worried.

"His mother, she's the key. She has cancelled checks from him with his bank on them. They are sitting on her desk. She lives in New Jersey, you can get her to bring them to a court. Subpoena her and the checks."

"That's crazy, she'd never bring them."

"She will, she'd be afraid not to. Besides she feels guilty covering for her son even though she wants him to have the children."

Three hours had passed. My head was feeling foggy right around the brain area. Time to call it quits.

Lou followed through. Two months later a subpoena was issued to Jillian's ex-mother-in-law requesting all papers her son had sent her. Jillian called and told me that her ex-in-law had brought the checks. More importantly, the address on the checks was on "E" street in Ramona, California.

Lou contacted the police in Ramona and they went to that address. By this time President Carter had signed the bill making parental abduction an indictable offense.

"Nancy, will I see my children this week?" Jillian anxiously asked.

"I don't see it, Jillian. I don't know why, but there will be a delay. It's okay, you will see them within the next few weeks. And Jillian, they will all remember you."

The call came in from Lou:

"The police found the apartment empty. He and the kids moved the day before. But we're lucky, he told a neighbor where he was moving. Hawaii, to the big island. I'm going to the judge and asking for a warrant for his arrest. With luck the Hawaii police will arrest him." (For Further recountings of Lou Masterbone, and to see how a police officer feels about working with a psychic, see appendix B).

Two days later on a Monday morning, Jillian called.

"Nancy, it's Jillian. Lou got the warrant. Do you think we're near the end?"

"This is it Jillian, you will see your children on Friday at 4:00 PM sharp. They will walk under an arch with a clock right above."

"Seriously, you think it's over?"

"Jillian, I am as sure as I can be the way I do things. I never know until it happens, but I feel strongly that I am seeing what is going to occur. You are your children will be reunited this Friday."

Jillian flew out and landed in Hawaii Friday morning. The phone rang at 10PM.

"Is Nancy there? This is Jillian's mother."

"Hi, it's me. How's Jillian?"

"She wants you to know the police arrested Joe and took the children in to a youth holding center. She was brought there and stood facing an archway with a clock overhead. At exactly 4:00 PM her three children walked under the arch and into her arms. We can't thank you enough."

"I didn't do it. Everyone did. I'm so happy for her, and for you."

Hanging up, the tears flowed and flowed. It was a total of 14 months since she had seen her children. I knew that there would be many adjustments and prices to pay for the damage to these innocent children. Many things have since happened to these children of a broken trust, and to their mother. That is another story. For the moment, though, their tears were of relief and joy. Sometimes justice does occur.

The following month my daughter, Rebecca, and I were in court. If you saw the film Kramer vs. Kramer, then you saw where we were.

And you also saw the true story about the lawyer who won custody of his son. He was standing in the hall, representing Gil. I never understood how he could allow the claims Gil made about me to be on paper for a child to eventually know. Barry Birbrower, friend and lawyer was talking to Gil's lawyer when he called me over.

We spoke for about 5 minutes, the words didn't seem important, just everyday conversation. Strange stuff while waiting for outsiders who will decide your life for you. Gil's lawyer excused himself and went to talk with Gil. Then he and Barry spoke alone. Then Barry took me aside. It was like a formal dance, only I didn't know the steps. Barry was smiling as he spoke:

"He dropped the case. He knew he didn't stand a chance. We were well prepared. I know a great restaurant, my treat."

Barry is one of the most unusual lawyers I've met. Heart and soul are part of everything he did for us. He never sent a bill, yet he spent two years working to free us from our nightmare.

Justice was really cooking that year.

(For Jillian's comments, see Appendix A)

NANCY WITH JESSE, REBECCA, RAMONA THE DOG AND SWEETIE PIE

(Star-Herald photo)

Psychic says powers are helping gift

'I was kidded about being a witch'

— Local news —

By PATTY PAUGH
Staff Writer

MOUNT OLIVE — Nancy Fuchs knew she was moving to New Jersey even before her husband decided to change jobs.

Nancy, a psychic who has accepted her talents for the past six years, was giving her husband a reading when she realized they would be leaving their home in Westchester, N.Y.

"I told him he would leave his other job and we would buy a house by a lake," she said. "I said, 'We're moving to New Jersey.'"

By that time, her husband was accustomed to her unusual powers, she says, so he wasn't surprised when they purchased a large stone house near Budd Lake — one Nancy had described to a realtor.

But not everyone is used to her abilities, or even believes she has them. Because she had visions of events before they happened, she says "I was always kidded about being a witch."

"It made everybody on edge. There was little understanding that it

was a gift to help people prepare for things," she said.

The lively 37-year-old woman has lived here for about two years, where she cares for her two children and stray cats.

Although she knew she had unusual powers since she was a child — foretelling events and picking up thoughts — she says she only tried to develop them in the past six years after she was crippled with back pain and facing several spinal operations.

"My husband took me to a psychic and I didn't believe in that at that time. He (the psychic) told me that I was a psychic and not to deny my powers anymore. He told me to go home and cure myself," she said.

"Later I did something very un-characteristic for me. I put my hands on my back and said, 'If there's a God, heal me.'"

Her pain disappeared and she began experimenting with her talents and learning to discipline her

thoughts. "A good psychic has to have an organized mind," she said.

Since then, she's experimented with her powers, and volunteers some of her time to the police.

In fact, some of the most skeptical people she meets are detectives, but she doesn't resent their suspicion.

"I think somebody would be a fool not to be a skeptic," she said.

Even the most hard-nosed cops realize she's not a fake when she tells them about crimes they're investigating. Now she works with police at least five hours a week.

But that's only a slice of her 60-hour work week. Nancy also does race horses through holistic medicine, writes lyrics, teaches parapsychology courses and gives readings.

Her skills are profitable; she charges $40 per hour for a reading and averages $100 to practice her medicine on equine clients.

In a reading, she delves into a person's past and future. "I talk to

them and tell them things about themselves. They don't have to talk, but I ask them to let me know if I'm on the right track," she said.

She analyzes a person to see if the physical, mental, emotional and spiritual elements are integrated. If people with positive energy are turned into destructive and negative tendencies in their personalities, she says.

"People who deny their own abilities have really destructive tendencies. People have to learn to be constructive by letting their guards down and enjoying their gifts," she said. "I work on a one-to-one basis. You can really alter the world with the way people think, feel and act."

Nancy believes that everyone has psychic abilities, which they ignore. People block out messages that are coming into their minds momentarily when they are with other people, she said. By not exploring these ideas, they never learn if the thoughts are justified, she maintains.

By developing her instincts by using intuition and predictions, "I want to show people how easy it really is," she says.

NEW JERSEY HERALD, OCT. 30, 1981

CHAPTER TWO
A MIRACLE HAPPENS

My greatest gratification as a human being is to have my gifts used to relieve suffering and strengthen lives. I think back on what brought me to realize that the strange powers accorded me are truly a blessing. This realization began on June 27th of 1975.

Since May 19, 1963 I had been in severe pain, had extensive spinal surgery, wore a body brace and had not recovered use of my left leg reflexes and muscle power since the nerve injuries were extensive and not regenerating. In desperation I was taken by my second husband, Jim, to see a psychic in Brooklyn. I was so terrified at the prospect of seeing a psychic that I spent the night dreaming of fires burning down my house.

I walked into a Brooklyn apartment and met the first person who openly acknowledged the world within. The psychic was sitting at a kitchen table eating dinner. He looked like a guy I would expect to meet on a street in Brooklyn. A melting pot look, maybe Jewish, or Italian, dark hair, dark eyes, light skin and a very normal looking face. I was waiting to meet someone who stood out in a crowd, caftan and crystal ball. He had neither. What he did have was a tape recorder and blank tape. Because I was able to hear the session years later on that precious tape, I too tape all my sessions for my clients.

The psychic did not tell me anything about others and there were no concrete details about things to come. Instead he approached me in the one way needed. He spoke of my fears and the energy blocks that prevented me from healing. He mirrored my inner truth so clearly that I could no longer hide. I went home and prayed for help to relieve the pain. I was given a miracle. I woke up pain free and that is how I remained for the first year.

Exactly one year later the pain returned, not as intense, more manageable, for now I was meditating. My inner teacher had returned from my childhood in full technicolor and I was no longer two dimensional. I started to give readings and healings. All of this with the loving guidance of a voice that called himself Ezekiel. He taught me for three years. I was told I was being prepared for my path. It was during this time that I was giving a reading in deep trance (I did trance work for the first three years) to my husband Jim.

He was asking me about his work. I told him, "In November you will lose your job, but don't worry. I see a man, short, very white skin, black hair. He is flying in from Germany. He is reorganizing his company. He will offer you a position. The job he will offer is better than the one you now have. Your present boss is a liar and a thief. You trust him, I don't. Anyhow, your new offer will start you at $21, 000, but we will move...to New Jersey! Oh well." "Where will we live?" "Near a lake and a place called Eagle Rock, and a Wolf Road. Our house will be huge...four huge bedrooms, giant living rooms..." "How will we afford this?" At the time I said this we lived in a four-room house. "I don't know, I only see..." another vision came to view... I saw my husband walking away with a much shorter woman with long dark hair. I knew right then it meant we would be apart. I was shocked, didn't say anything, just stored it away. Jim was not someone who would even look at another woman. That meant that we would be separated and then he would find someone else. I quickly ended the session. Jim could not read my poker face. Years ago my family would play cards for hours and I would show my hand on my face with eager excitement. Then I played in Las Vegas and hooked up with a professional player who taught me not to be read. It came in handy that night but since the armor had been torn down I was not comfortable playing games. I went to bed early and soon the image faded into the background along with many others.

November came and went. Jim still worked at the same place. I found him being drawn closer to his boss and trusting him with all the confidential material he was working on. I stayed quiet and unhappy and no longer distrusted what the inner voice said. I didn't know how to help Jim see what was so clear to me. We were having many difficulties with that. Jim was having trouble feeling comfortable with the ever present people who sought my help. He was angry when they would ask if he could give readings. Soon he stopped participating and when I held classes he stopped attending, telling me he knew he had ego issues but he couldn't help it. We were parting before my eyes. My vision came back and now I didn't hide from it. I could see how competitive Jim was in sports, in work, in play. Everything was to prove himself. I was competitive too, but with only one person, me. I wanted to stretch down to the endless, limitless universe. I wanted and still do, to feel myself as Spirit. Nothing else, pure energy, but I don't want to wait for death to teach me that, I want it here and now on earth.

Another November came around and this time all things shifted. Jim came home very upset. "I was fired." His look was of disbelief. "Why?" "The president accused me of taking money and covering up a huge mistake." Jim's face was pale gray. Along with the accusation the knowledge sank in that we had known this would happen and he simply helped it along. "You know who framed you don't you?" I spoke quietly and as gently as I could. I knew it would all turn out all right and we would even move to New Jersey. The prediction was happening exactly one year later. "Yes. John, my boss." I had never seen him cry and didn't now, but he came as close as he could. My whole being rose like a bird ready to fly to great heights. The self was gone and in its place came the inner being and it spoke, "Remember the rest of what I said. You don't have to do a thing. Work will come to you quickly." Because the prediction had started to occur, Jim held onto this belief. So did I. Four years before this he was laid off in the construction industry and would not seek any work. No amount of pleading or coaxing would lift his depression and I worked hard to get by with two children and unemployment checks. Eight months later his father brought him into the firm he now worked at. Only my reawakened psychic gifts kept my fears in check. Normally I would have been upset and believed in a repeat of what we had been through. These wonderful doors were now wide open.

The next week Jim received a call from a company that was looking to reorganize. It was a German firm and the president was flying over to change the structure of the company. They wanted to interview Jim. He hung up elated, so did I, I knew what the President looked like, what salary Jim would make, $6,000 more than he had at the last place. Jim looked puzzled.

"What's the funny look for?"

"Their company is in the Empire State Building in New York, they're not in New Jersey."

"Oh well, most of it is true and you will get the job. Good for you."

The phone rang again. This time it was the president of Jim's previous firm. He was apologizing for firing him. They found evidence against John. Jim was glad, but no longer wanted to deal with them. He rang off, confidence fully restored.

The next Monday Jim went on his interview with joy. He came home and greeted me with a very peculiar look. "I got the job and they are starting me at $21, 000." "Good, when do you start?" "In January." "Why January?" "They are moving their headquarters to New Jersey and they want me there."

Jim took a room near the job while I kept up my work from home, went house hunting and kept the house available for prospective buyers. He would not let me look in the county where I knew the house of my vision was. Every house we put a bid on for the next 5 months went sour. We could not buy any of them. One day I had had enough.

"Jim, if you are not willing to let me look we will never be together. This is insane. I can't keep taking days off and driving around Jersey searching."

He gave in. I picked up the phone and called a real estate agent in the one county he had kept me out of....Morris.

"Hi, I'm looking for a five-bedroom house. It has a back staircase leading from the kitchen to the outside that is painted green. It is one block from a lake near Eagle Rock and Wolf Road. It has the ugliest picture of Jesus I've ever seen."

"Mrs. Fuchs, where is this house you've seen?"

"I have no clue. That's why I'm calling you. It will be on the market for $100,000 or a few thousand under."

"Did you see it listed somewhere?"

"No. Listen, I'm sure this is strange to you, but I had a vision and I know it's real. As long as you get your commission, it doesn't really matter how I found out, does it?"

She called back with three houses, none of which she had seen. I drove out with a friend, Shannon and my children. We drove up to the first house and I said, "don't bother, this isn't it." In the next house we made it to the living room, where I said, "not this one either." As we drove to the third, we were passing a lake on the right when the realtor made a left and drove one block. Staring at us was a stone dwelling. Shannon and I shared the moment.

"This is it."

We walked in and looked through room after room, all spacious and strongly built. Through the kitchen and down the backstairs. The realtor could only say..."it's all painted green." We stopped to look in the tool room downstairs and there, hanging over the workbench was the last piece. The ugliest rendering I had ever seen of Jesus.

"Place my bid on the house for $79,000."

I didn't even call Jim, didn't need to. He had told me to go ahead if I found it. The broker responded: "79,000. I can't do that. It's listed for $98,000."

"Who are you working for? We can pass for a mortgage and we are ready to buy. Just tell them and see."

The next day she called to tell us the owners wouldn't even answer the bid.

"Fine, tell them $82,500 and it's our final bid." She did, and we closed on the house for that price in August of 1979. We were in New Jersey. Within three months the police would be knocking on my door.

※※※※※※

CHANNELING INFORMATION — As a child, Budd Lake resident Nancy Fuchs knew she was destined to be different because she had the ability to know and understand things — sometimes before they happened. Says Fuchs, "It's another place if information literally comes from and it comes to strongly in and through you that you just hurt it out."

Budd Lake woman opens the mind's barriers

By PEGGY WRIGHT
Staff Writer

BUDD LAKE — Nancy Fuchs was destined to be different — yet, whether she wanted to be or not.

While driving, the visions are strong, she would at times hear a sudden news broadcast although she had not turned the radio on. Once the news was that Charles had been born — a 1680. Fuchs reported to her mother when she returned them and

WHEN FUCHS mother discussed the news with co-workers the next day, she received astonished looks — the prince was not born, but his birth was announced several weeks later.

"When you say it, it's very hard for people to understand. You don't know beforehand what you're saying," Fuchs said.

house at Budd Lake.

"It's what we call channeling — information that doesn't come from a common part of us. It's another place the information literally comes from and it comes so strongly in and through you that you just hurt it out," she said.

Ten years ago, as a working psychic, Fuchs said she went to extremes coming out of Egypt to sign with Israel. The man was Anwar El-Sadat, who became president of Egypt as he worked forever.

Today, Fuchs works with a group of people who are representatives of various organizations at the United Nations. She must be cautious about giving details of her work, but predicts. There is a potential in people are born with the ability to perceive, but most create barriers against the perceptions and learn to ignore their "sixth sense," and Fuchs

"In your external senses you recognize that internally, you have started

Often she saw death lurking, as in a friend who died a year after Fuchs sensed he had a problem.

RATHER THAN alert, she learned to transmit a more peaceful message: I would mentally offer to help them.

"I don't like to just with ever to somebody and say, 'hey, you could save me. You're not well. That's crazy. So, I would rather send loving thoughts and healing. I think of the body internally, it image of them and then send a message that I am available if they need me," Fuchs said.

Fuchs, who was left with crushed nerves in her spine and leg.

Spinal surgery, extensive operations and a month in traction — the course of Fuchs life for 11 years after the incident. Although she still carried the pain was chronic and intense.

in the same sense. Images are stored along the body's circuits, so I don't know why some people are born with the ability to use it better. Most people build defenses against intuition," she said.

Dubbed a "freak," an "oddball," and ostracized as a child by people who feared her perceptions, Fuchs said she too tried to deny the perceptions.

WANTING A safe and controlled life at it, Fuchs loved ballet but studied nursing. At 15 a 200-pound patient "thought I was a chair and threw herself at me," said Fuchs, who was left with crushed nerves in her spine and leg.

mentally rebelled against.

"Everything I ever got psychically was so intense and powerful that whenever I said anything, everyone would find it and take 10 steps backward. It was like lightning shooting through," she said.

Fuchs went to the psychic who would later believe in herself and go home and heal herself.

"I went home, put my hands on my back and said, 'OK, God, if you're there, heal me."

FUCHS WOULD slowly not describe herself as a religious person, but the self-healing however "slowly," saved her and charged her life.

"That 200-pound woman changed my life. I ought to find her and kiss her, I would have just gone back and done ballet and nursed and that would have been it. At that time she did something, I find inconsolable," she said.

CHAPTER THREE
THE MIND'S
EYE VIEWS A CRIME

"I'm being robbed!"

I was picking up my chopsticks, ready for another mouthful of Ho Fun, when the vision blew across my mind.

Everyone looked at me. Joyce said "What?" looking at my handbag under the table.

"I mean my house is being robbed, not here. I just saw two men leaving out my bedroom window. It's too late to catch them, they fled. I'll deal with it when I get back."

I had been anxious all day, now I finally knew why. Comforted by the idea that there are people in the police department of Mt. Olive Township that I can call upon who would understand how I operate, I sat back ready to continue my lunch.

It was a relief to know why I had been anxious all day. Many years ago, my first roommate nicknamed me "Mary Sunshine". Helen, my roommate at my first nursing job, hated how I was so cheerful — "It's disgusting," she would groan — and I would just have to sing louder and louder to wake her for work. Even as a child, I ran outside to see the sun come up. This morning had been different.

In spite of the cheerful sounds of nature coming through my open window, I just wanted to turn over and go back to sleep. Anxiety poured through my body as soon as I started to drift to the surface. If only, inside me, there were a little blinking light, just like the walk sign on the street - only this would say "Intuition" or "Forget it; it's old fear."

The few times I had experienced severe anxiety as an adult, a feeling of fluid electricity would run from my lower spine down my legs. It would be such a strong surge, that I would feel my legs lose all strength and begin to buckle. Often when near someone in a lot of pain, I get this strange sensation. It terrifies me, but it also leaves me absolutely certain we are all connected. It's also been my warning of danger.

Lying in bed and being afraid to face the day was making me angry. I hate being afraid, particularly of something so nebulous as what's going on in my day. Getting angry at my fear usually helps me overcome all the weak and negative feelings. It's great, I get a lot done when I'm angry — but I notice I get a lot done when I'm happy, too. I've used anger and laughter as the vehicles to drive my pain away. I get this wondrous high when I'm pulling the pain along the winds of anger. Usually I reach a point where I see how silly I am, I crack up laughing at myself and it's over. But nothing shakes it on this day.

I convinced my eyes to look at the room. The soft shades of sand and muted royal blue greeted me. The bedroom was the first space I decorated. All my life I just parked myself wherever I landed and proceeded to play or work. A place was just a space of convenience. Now feelings of belonging, like a tree rooted, silently growing deeper in the search for nourishment had spread into my being.

The first day of our move I stared at the wooden floors that had been worn down with angry feet. Scratch marks were everywhere. The walls and ceiling were peeling off, only to show plaster beneath the old grey paint which used to be white.

The bedroom seemed sad and unloved. It must have tugged at a closed door inside my psyche. A new desire started to spread. I had to help the room. It was the first time I felt a need to help an inanimate being. As I stared a vision came to me. The walls had a wainscotting midway through and rectangular portions surrounded by white painted wood. In the interior boxes I suddenly saw a pattern of blue roses and taupe leaves. The exterior was an ivory shade. As I looked to the ceiling the same pattern appeared. "How am I ever going to do that?" My neck hurt at the thought of it.

On my mission to love the room, I found the perfect pattern in an English wallpaper. Having limited funds, I gulped at the price. Upon use, I discovered its self-pasted back wasn't staying on the wall. The store refunded me half the price and gave me wall paste. I put as much effort and determination into that room as if I were still at Lincoln Hospital, South Bronx, working in the Intensive Care Unit. That room needed my care and as stubborn as the walls were, I was their match. Covering the floor with a textured sand colored rug was easy. I pointed, paid and used it. It was worth it, the results were a soothing room to meditate in. Within months I was inspired to write poetry, and soon music began to take shape in my head. All for the love of a room.

A year after I had done that two men showed up at our door. Although bearing no striking resemblance to each other, they turned out to be father and son. The father was slim and introspective looking, quiet brown hair that sat gently and unobtrusively on his head. Brown rimmed glasses that helped quiet brown eyes greet me.

"Hello, I'm Mr. Peters and this is my son. When I was a young boy I stayed here every summer. My grandfather had the place built for him."

His son, blond, blue-eyed, wide-face and muscular joined in. "My father's told me so much about the place."

"I've been wondering about this house. Every room has a different look to it," I said.

"That's because my grandfather travelled all around the world. He originally worked for Burroughs as an engineer. He was one of the designers of the adding machine. He then went and sold the concept to the world. He designed each room to represent a different country he stayed in and loved. I would love to see it again and show my son."

I turned to the father, delighted at the opportunity.

" Great, let's start with the master bedroom."

He stepped in and stopped. His quiet demeanor changed rapidly. His slim body turned into a wiry frame of excitement: "It hasn't changed, it's exactly the same. Wallpaper, rug, paint, all the same. How could that be?"

That was an interesting visit.

The bedroom was even more special after that visit, so I was surprised at my desire to hide from the day and the room. I became even more nervous suspecting that part of me knew something that wouldn't tell my conscious mind. For me, anger always gets rid of fear. Anger at being afraid seems to conquer and calm my terror. How dare I or anyone make me afraid? Off go the covers, pad over to the kitchen, make a cup of coffee, sip it, and place in a tiny corner of the mind the fact that something might happen that I won't like. Besides, today my children and I have a lunch date with Joyce.

By noon I started to hunt for my kids. Jesse was still in his pajamas playing Dungeons and Dragons. This was his latest craze.

"Why do I have to get dressed?"

"Get dressed," I said, "we leave in 5 minutes. It's the third time I've asked you and the last. You can go in your pajamas."

Rebecca must have changed her outfit three times until she got the "right look." She has an amazing flair for the use of design. Even when she was three years old, she would borrow some of my clothes to complete the fashion statement she wanted to create.

Ten minutes later, the three of us were outside. My blue knight awaited us. In 1979 my brand new Pacer caught fire the week we were to move to New Jersey. Necessity brought out an ability to bargain I never saw in me before. Needing money for the move, I fought to get the best deal. It turned out to be better than just saving money. The blue Chevy Caprice Station Wagon only failed to run well twice in its 180,000 mile life. Both times occurred in the driveways of two of my best friends. One knew how to fix it, the other knew how to call a mechanic and pass the time playing Parchesi. After that I nicknamed it the Blue Knight.

Rebecca stood by my side as I looked up at the house. Eyes closed, I began to image our stone house. As my focus increased, I spread an image of the whitest light I could imagine over it. Why can't I get the light around my bedroom? Tried again and again with no luck. The image was stuck. Darkness surrounded the back of the house in my mind. I turned to my daughter.

"Rebecca honey, could you pretend you see white light all around the house?"

"Sure mommy."

She stood still, eyes focused on the house. About two minutes went by when she turned to me with a puzzled expression; "I can almost get white all around the house. From top to bottom I painted it white."

Right arm stretched out, finger aimed toward the left.

"The bottom left is dark."

"You sure?"

"Yes, mommy, why?"

"Oh, the same thing happened for me. My bedroom is dark. The morning fear poured into me like a gulp of lightning.

"That's okay sweetheart, you did a great job. Let's go eat with Joyce. Wonder where we'll eat?"

My smile was one of those, "smile for the children" jobs. I know better, children feel the truth. I know better than to confuse their reality but fear makes me stupid. So does guilt, and I wanted my children to have a day away from the problems that we lived with. Life had been scary for them recently. Jesse's dad, Rebecca's stepfather, and I were in the process of tearing down what we had built. A divorce was in the works.

"Are you kids sitting way in the back?"

"Of course we are," giggled Rebecca.

Grateful for the distance between us, I thought about my beloved bedroom. Music, kids' chatter and truck wheels all felt miles away from my ears. Anxiety lingered in my gut like a meal of lead. I cruised down the familiar residential section of Morristown, and finally into Madison where Joyce lived. She was moving to Arizona and we tried to see each other as much as possible before the move. I pulled into the driveway by a white and pale blue Victorian house. Joyce's black Saab was standing in the driveway. We pulled up alongside.

"Hi sweetheart, look at you Rebecca, don't you look beautiful."

My girlfriend's long dancer's arms hugged Rebecca. At 13 years of age, Rebecca stood tall with the grace of a young gazelle. Her long, thick auburn hair and her sculpted beauty reminded one painter of "Botticelli; he would have loved her." Next came Jesse's turn. An eight year old going through hurts, he managed to pull away and cling at the same time. Every time I looked at him I prayed that the humor would return to his blue-gray eyes.

We decided to go to one of our favorite Chinese restaurants. The Mayflower is a hangout in Morristown for vegetarians. It has a regular menu for the rest of the world and a vegetarian menu for us folks. Ordering food was easy for me. It's all great. In case you want to double check on the accuracy of this food review, it's on Morris Avenue.

My reverie was broken by Joyce asking, "Do you want to leave? Why don't you call the police?"

"No, nothing should spoil our fun. This was supposed to be a day off."

They all looked at me. If I was being robbed, do something. If it was my imagination, it's a bizarre one because it comes equipped with details of other peoples lives, looks, habits, etc. Being stubborn sometimes has benefits. Joyce knew it was pointless to continue to get me to do something when I didn't want to.

We finished lunch and returned to our car in Joyce's driveway. She left me with a, "Call me and let me know. Be careful."

As we headed home, I prepared myself mentally to carefully enter the house. Parking brakes on, I turned to look way back and spoke to the kids.

"Okay listen to me. This is important. Do exactly what I ask of you. Just follow behind me, do not touch anything in the house. Even the front door. Okay, time to go in, follow me."

The three of us must have looked like ducks on an outing. I looked with all three eyes. First the front door. My physical vision showed the door wasn't tampered. My psychic eye showed no change in energy. I hoped both visions were accurate.

Years before I had dated a man named Steve. Steve worked at one time repossessing cars. He showed me how to pick a lock and how to know when one has been played with. It has come in handy a few times in life. Unfortunately it was always because someone wanted something. The last time I looked at a lock was in the Bronx in 1968. I lived in an apartment on the Grand Concourse, 3rd floor with a boyfriend. We went out at 6:30PM for dinner and arrived back at 8:30PM. Key ready to go in the lock I stopped.

"Don't touch the lock, someone's paid us a visit."

He stopped and I showed him the scratch marks. George, my boyfriend, actually had one of those things called hankies. I used it to open the door. We were greeted to a mess. Drawers open, Nikon camera and jewelry stolen, they had even taken shirts. It was how I learned to trust my feelings, and to get insurance.

We continued our column of three into the hall. We walked on our chocolate colored shag rug that showed every bit of dirt that even came near it. No matter how often it was cleaned, it was filthy. A big comfortable rug, stained with "I won't bring any more food into the living room" stains. Beige corduroy couch sat under a window. Only a year old, it looked like it had been there for decades. It too had grown roots. Two of our cats, Sweetie Pie and Mu, were lying there.

"Kids, go join the cats and keep them company. I don't know where the two men went other than my bedroom. Please just sit there until I'm done checking." "Why?" said my two baby ducks. "Just sit there for 5 minutes. I'll be right back. No one is here now but us." I hoped my intuition was correct. I walked through the living room into the hall and stopped. To the left my bedroom door stood closed. I had left it open. To the right is a staircase leading up to the second floor.

Ramona was waiting at the top of the steps. Our beautiful mutt had come to us through a local shelter. Badly abused by her previous owner she had a broken hip that had not been properly repaired, seizures on an almost daily basis, and the sweetest face. She was part collie, part shepherd, about 45 lbs. of shy love. The children adored her. She never hid her fear, she barked at every new sound and smell. Now her eyes were as dark as tar. Her tail was swooped down and held tight. She always barked, even at us. She was so scared she was quiet. Slowly she came to me.

"Ramona, it's mommy. It's okay now. No one hurt you, did they?"

"No," a strange voice inside my head answered.

Years of working with animals plus the loss of one very dear cat when I didn't trust the voice, has taught me to listen and believe. I relate that story in the chapter on animals.

As I sat holding Ramona, my right hand stayed on top of her head while the left stroked her. Closing my eyes to see, I was rewarded quickly. Vision and sound internally took over. I believe I was looking out from Ramonas' eyes. I had become her for a moment. My palms opened in a gesture of healing. I prayed: "God, I ask to be a channel of light and love for all concerned, especially for Ramona whose fear is so prevalent." Next, I could hear sounds. They seemed to be coming from my bedroom. Her terror leapt out of her mouth, the barks must have been loud. She came running down the steps. Seeing through her eyes, the bedroom door began to close. Vision faded. That's what happened. I laughed out loud,

"Ramona, you're incredible. They were afraid of the big angry dog. I'm glad they locked the door. It would have been terrible if they hurt you." She was quivering, letting her fear out.

"Go to the kids sweetheart, they'll take care of you."

She turned and marched into the living room, tail a little bit higher, a hint of a wag started as she heard Rebecca's voice calling her.

I hate this, hate this, hate this. Why do people like making others afraid? Wake up, anger, and help me. I'm frozen at the door. Deep breath, good, another one, put your hand on the door. Good, now open it. Two visions jumped up. To my eyes my bedroom was still the special place. Bed unmade, standard procedure, years of being a nurse cured me of the desire to make beds. Closet doors closed, no dresser drawers open. My body knew different. Intruders, call the police. Take a look first and see what happened. It's over, it won't happen again. Oh yeah, that's exactly what I said after someone raped me. Two years later, lying in my bed, an intruder attacked me. He got away and I was so upset I ran into the arms of my wonderful knight, Gil. How psychic can you get? Six months later he slapped my face, two years later we divorced. Boy, could I pick them. I hate intruders, they mess my head up so much that I walk into worse and worse.

I let my eyes relax and consciously opened my third eye. Focus with intent, drop fear, drop fury, go dead calm. Ready, aim, see... the room was in chaos. Waves of light no longer flowed throughout. Jagged lines of muddy colors scorched the air. Patterns of anger and resentment hovered over my head. Follow the muddy brick road to the window. The lock on the window was broken. Remember to repair the lock. Stay calm, stay cool.

As I stared at the window two shapes showed themselves coming through a mist inside my head. Two young men, both with dark unkempt hair. One I felt was Dean, a young man who once did some sheetrock for us a few years back. He was easy to identify; slight of build, pock marked cheeks and sloped shoulders. But mostly, just a feel of familiarity. The other I did not recognize, but the name John popped up in my head as I continued to stare. His image was not clear. I can refocus that later, I thought. As I watched, Dean climbed on John's shoulders and pried open the window. Window open, Dean jumped into the room and walked over to my jewelry box sitting on my oak dresser. It's a good thing I no longer own any valuable jewelry. Watching him open up the doors of the box and take my new watch, I checked my emotions behind my vision. He had found the only piece worth more than $100. He didn't lift the lid on top where all my earrings are kept. He left them alone.

I walked over to my dresser to double check the vision. Watch was gone. Okay, where is it? My watch was sitting on a dresser in a bedroom. The voice I was used to as the voice of truth, said, "at John's girlfriends apartment in Kings Village." Kings Village is the apartment complex next to Eagle Rock.

In a drawer near the jewelry box I had kept the start of a coin collection for Jesse. He loved money and was fascinated by our trip to the US Mint, cash registers, coin shops and my money. They took the kids coin collection. How nasty. "They are spending it on hot dogs," came the voice. That's so insulting and stupid. Nothing else was missing of my jewelry, probably because all the real stuff had been stolen years before, and since then I never wanted to own any. Again I checked, coins were gone.

I looked around the room, following the discord. We had two closets side by side. One was Jim's, one mine. Facing them, the left side of my body was being tugged towards Jim's closet. Nothing seems missing. Trust yourself, keep looking. Then I remembered. The rifle is gone. No, I hate this. Bad enough Jim insisted on having it here. Bullets, where are the bullets? Whew, still on the top shelf. Shaking, there was no comfort to the idea that I no longer had to see that weapon of destruction. Men created it, men bought them and men stole them. Do we women ever get a say? Or children? Where are all the gentle, non-violent men? Come on, stand up with us and legislate weapons out of existence.

I watched as Dean jumped out the window handing the watch to John. They walked up the hill to Eagle Rock Apartments.

"Okay kids, you can move. Just don't go in my room."

"Why?"

"Some men came in through the bedroom window and took some of our belongings. Jesse, they took your coins."

A leg kicking hard was his only response.

"Why can't we go in?"

"Because that is the only place they went and the police will look for evidence and fingerprints in that room. We don't want to confuse them. Do you know that Ramona kept them from going into the rest of the house. Give the wonder dog extra special hugs."

I walked over to the phone.

"Mt. Olive Police Department."

"I'm reporting a burglary that took place in my home this afternoon while I was out. Please send someone over."

Usually the police call me, today it's my turn to call them. When I first moved to Budd Lake I met the first female police officer of Mt. Olive, Michele Bochenek. She taught karate to children two miles down the road from our house. My son Jesse signed up.

One day Michele approached me after class. Having read

about my work with finding missing animals she asked if I would help on a police matter.

"We had a rape in town. Could you pick anything up on it?"

Immediately my thoughts turned into words, "If you have a suspect, does he have red hair? Did he pick up a large rock and hit her on the head?"

"Would you mind if my superior speaks to you about it?"

I soon learned that answers would not come readily, not until the officer in charge would give his approval.

The next week Michele introduced Detective Ross English as her superior. He asked me to repeat what I had told her. Again, no answer, just, "Can I come to your office tomorrow with my partner?"

The next afternoon Det. English and Det. Dave Johnson (not his real name) sat in my office asking me for the third time what I had seen. Then Ross said, "We have two suspects with red hair, how can we tell which one?"

I stood up and limped across the room, sat down and said, "That one."

"How did you do that? He walks just like you did. "

Now we became Ross, Dave and Nancy looking at cases. That afternoon they left my office to return later with some unsolved, still open cases. Now its my turn for help.

My address and name given to the dispatcher, I hung up and waited. No bell at our front door, so I listened for the sound of our metal lion banging against the huge wooden front door. About five minutes passed before I answered the door.

"Hi, I'm Nancy. Thank you for coming. Let me show you where it occurred."

Ramona was back to normal, she barked non-stop until I asked the children to take her upstairs with them. Out of sight of the scary new person she would quiet down.

The officer and I entered what used to be my sanctuary. He walked in and I showed him the window.

"This lock was fine when I left, and in place."

"Hello, where's everybody?"

An unmistakable voice leaped across the living room.

"In here, follow the sound of my voice. Hi Dave."

"You know each other?" the officer asked as Dave brought his full 240lb hulk into the room. His shock of blond hair and round cherub features softened his 6'1" frame into a non-threatening look.

"Sure I know Nancy. Just let her tell you everything she knows, no matter how odd it sounds to you. And take it all down, don't leave out anything."

Dave was bending over by the window.

"Why didn't you call the department, we would have been right over. I heard it on the radio."

"I didn't want to bother you."

"How were they able to break into your home?"

"I couldn't put light around the bedroom. They must have planned it for days."

Dave just nodded in understanding, the other officer looked more bewildered.

"Do you see what happened?" Dave was watching me pace the room.

"Yes, it's coming in pretty clear."

"Okay, start writing what she says."

The officer had his pad and pen ready for action. Not even a questioning look. I was impressed. He must be curious; I bet he plays poker well.

Barefoot and darting from window to dresser to closet I spoke;

"There were two young men. One stood on the others shoulders to open the window. They both came in. Both are dark haired, Dean is slim, the other, John is chunky and short. He's got a girlfriend who he gave my watch to. I want it back. It's on her dresser in Kings Village Apartments."

"Do you have all that?" Dave questioned the cop.

"Yes."

"Okay Nancy, go on."

"John watched the hallway and Dean opened my jewelry box. He found the coins first and the watch. The coins are collectors items. Okay, now he's at my closet. Yuk, he looked at my things. Nothing of interest. He's at Jim's closet now. He found the shotgun, or rifle, I really don't know what that beast is, just as they heard Ramona bark and her paws thumping away down the stairs. The 2nd guy John closed the door, and they both left immediately through the window."

"Do you know what make, what caliber." The officer was determined to get details.

"Not a chance. I refuse to be able to learn those things. I'll ask Jim when he gets home and I'll call it in. Ready for more?"

"Sure."

"The 1st guy to come in was a kid who worked for us last year. His name is Dean. John is his Joe. Older than him. Dean is slim, dark haired, very narrow face. Mother lives in Eagle Rock apartments. John's girlfriend lives in Kings Village Apartments, he is shorter than Dean by two inches, also dark hair and light skin but broader all around with about 20 lbs. extra weight. They steal locally on a regular basis. Nice kids, what a waste."

"I think I know these two." Dave looked thoughtful.

"You do? Good, that means I may get back my things. Loose the gun in the evidence room forever please. Where were we?"

I was waiting for the film in the air to continue. Just like a hologram museum only these images moved a lot. Film started to roll...

"Dean took the shotgun and put it in his mothers' apartment in her attic. I can see him hiding it there. She's not home yet. Will be soon. John gave my watch to his girlfriend. What nerve, they used the rare coins to buy franks. And me a vegetarian. Idiots, I wish they hadn't spent them, they can't be recovered. Oh well, nothing I can do about it now. I think that's all I've got."

Dave and the officer left after details of the value on the items were written into the report. By this time it was 3:00 PM and the theft had occurred at 12:30.

Jim came home from work at 6:30 PM and we went over the scene again and again until I walked over to a brass lamp hanging on a wall directly above the jewelry box.

"He didn't wear gloves" I turned to Jim.

Joining me he looked; "There's a print here," he said.

"That's one of theirs. I can feel its energy is different. Let's take it down and bring it over." Carefully putting it in a plastic bag we took the lamp to the police. It was now 7:30 PM.

Walking into the rundown police station is an experience. I've been in many, and this is the worst. You walk into a tiny room with a dispatcher behind a window. Everything in the room is old and faded, even the posters. You can see a tiny bathroom to the left up three steps. Dirty and ugly, it may turn off many to even report something, but to work there would be much harder. Probably discourages the officers from hanging around.

I requested to speak to Ross English, and after speaking on the phone, the dispatcher buzzed open the inner sanctum door. Down short and twisted corridors we strode. Every time I walked through these halls I felt as if I was in a poorly pieced jigsaw puzzle that didn't quite fit. Truth is the police station in Mt. Olive is an embarrassment to the police. It's a makeshift bunch of trailers strung together however they would fit. Everyone who is there gets to see who is walking through. There is no privacy.

Passing Lt. Drake's office, his ever present unlit pipe in hand, we exchanged smiles and waves. Always liked him, he never seemed to be a part of any of the petty problems or corrupt dealings.

We walked through two offices, had to say, "excuse me," in order to get to the detective bureau. The bureau is long and narrow. Three desks in a row with a narrow passage that holds a copy machine. Ross' desk was third in line. Two chairs were waiting by his side and I quickly landed in the one near him.

"I got the report from Dave and we had four search warrants within the hour from the judge."

"I then called Deans' mother and told her to bring her son in for questioning. I didn't tell her what it was about. They came in near 5:00. I told Dean that there was an eye witness to the burglary he and his friend John committed this afternoon. At first he didn't believe me. So I told him the eye witness followed him and saw him put the shotgun in his mothers' attic."

"At that point he confessed to everything. Told me he climbed in the window, took your watch, coin and gun and got out before the dog could tear him apart. He didn't ask how anyone could see him go into his mothers' attic. When I told him that the eye witness saw him do it, he and his mother took Dave and I to their apartment and retrieved the gun."

Dave then took another officer and went to John's girlfriend's apartment in Kings Village. When they got to the door, she stood there telling them they can't come in without a search warrant. So they handed her the warrant and went in. Dave went right over to her bedroom dresser and picked up your watch, told her she was in trouble for receiving stolen property and left. By the time he returned here, (the apartments were both less than 5 minutes from the police station) we received a call from John. He was at a phone booth near the Dairy Queen, begging us not to shoot him. He confessed on the phone and asked if he could please come in. That's about 8 hours from start to finish. That's what happens when you have an eye witness who sees clearly."

(For further recountings of Ross English on this case and his comments on some other interesting work with Nancy, see Appendix C)

CHAPTER FOUR
INTUITION DENIED

Tomorrow I'm getting married...again. Jim has been good to me, better than Gil. Funny, I'll be a June bride but I don't think it's anything like the stories I heard. Nancy why can't you say no?

Looking down at my swollen belly, alive with a wild child yet to be born, Jim's words spoken last week clung to a speck of my heart.

"The union agreed to cover your medical costs if we get married. Find out what we have to do and we'll go to the mayor's office next week and do it."

I kept running through his words hoping to spot a bit of love in there. I told myself, "He must love me, he wanted a child with me, we planned our baby. But he only said I love you once since you've know him, Nancy. And you've known him for 5 years. Why are you doing this," I thought to myself.

Not getting any answers but fog, I opened the screen door and awaited our visitors. It was 1974 and we were dressing in the style of the day. Bob and Betty arrived first. Bob was tall, lanky and midwestern in his rhythm. His dungarees were topped by an Indonesian shirt, same style Jim wore, the thinnest of white cotton with colorful flowers embroidered down the front. Betty wore flowers, in her hair, on her shirt and embroidered on her dungarees. Their Malamute came bounding into our small four room converted barn. Her brother Fang was on a run outside. We had bought Fang from the same breeder. My two cats, Sweetie Pie and Michael, her son, were outside. Michael was eleven months old and no matter what we tried to do, Sweetie Pie continued to nurse him. She also wanted to teach him to stalk, which is probably what she was doing at the time. She had tried many times but Michael steadfastly loved every living thing he came in contact with. He was beautiful to look at too. Where Sweetie Pie was white from head to toe with blotches of black and grey tiger stripes, Michael was a long haired, radiant black cat with a gentle grace about him.

Two more couples came from New York City, all friends of Jim's whom I had an acquaintance with. Tim and Jan were the "swingers." At least he was. He was known to "try" all of his friends' female companions. No one seemed to mind. Actually that's probably because they had none. Then there was Greg and Beth. He was a professor of Eastern Languages. When they all got together they would drink beer, pass a joint and talk their own language of a 20 year friendship. Being shy had made it difficult to enter into any groups that didn't easily make room for newcomers, and this group was tight.

It was now three o'clock and lunch was over. Bob got up to walk his dog.

"Bob, if you don't have a leash we do. There's one right by the door. Michael and Pie are outside. Please put the leash on." I started to get up and he was gone, without the leash.

Bob ignored me as everyone did. He sauntered out while his dog bounded towards something with great determination. The screen door was left ajar. One day Jim will fix the spring on it.

Michael came running in and onto my lap. Michael, what happened baby.

"She killed me."

The words screamed in my head. Michael dashed out of my lap and down into the unfinished basement.

"Jim call the vet. Michael is hurt."

"Why are you carrying on. He looks fine."

"Calm down Nancy, you're just excited." Jims' audience echoed.

"Call the vet now." My voice took on a tone I only remembered having when I worked in the Intensive Care Unit or psychiatry. Down in the basement I spotted Michael. Cradled in my arms, I carried him back up. Rebecca was now in the room.

"Mommy is Michael all right?"

"No Bec, and I don't know if he will be. He may die."

"Oh stop it. Rebecca, he'll be fine. Your mom is just upset."

"You are not an expert."

"Neither are you, and you have no right to upset your daughter."

Jims' friend Bill was on a roll. He liked to be kind daddy.

"And you have no right to whitewash what has happened. I want Rebecca prepared to maybe have to say good-bye to Michael. She loves him just as much as I do."

Michael tell me what's wrong.

"My lung is punctured."

"Jim, Michael's lung is punctured, I don't know what to do. Hurry, is the vet answering?

Two hours went by, Michael in my arms, Sweetie Pi now staying by my side, and Rebecca gently stroking him.

When the phone rang relief set in. Now at last there is help. Jim, Rebecca, Michael and I left Jims' friends at our home and drove the ten miles to the animal hospital. X-ray taken:

"I can't see any problem but if you want I'll observe him through the night."

"I don't understand it. His lung is punctured. He told me, I can feel it. I know it's true. Can't you do something?"

"No, if I operate and nothing is there, it's risking his life for nothing. I can't chance it."

We left with my heart weighing a ton. I knew I'd never see that adorable love bucket again. He even helped mice. Birds fed right next to him. He was our wonder kitten, even his mother cried tears at his birth.

Not again, dear God please don't do this. Save Michael, it's not fair.

As we drove home I was re-captured by a time in Puerto Rico when I was pregnant with Rebecca. Little Bit was a tiny underweight kitten, black with white paws that we rescued. I fed her fresh food and vitamins. Within a year she had a coat that glowed with health. When she became pregnant we commiserated and compared bellies. We napped together. Ten days after I gave birth, she gave birth to a two inch kitten, but she had more kittens and they couldn't come out. Gil was a doctor, and he took her in to his lab rather than to a vet. I was ill and couldn't lift my head from the pillow so I wasn't totally aware. I was busy trying to nurse a baby and unbeknownst to my mind, my body was dying of massive infections. Gil operated and anesthetized her. The operation was a success but the patient died. On our first anniversary. It was the death knoll for our marriage. Maybe that's why I can't believe it's okay. Maybe I am wrong. So scared I can't have a good life. Michael, I hope I'm just crazy. Back home we said good-bye to everyone. I went to lay down and there I stayed until the phone rang at 6AM.

"Who is it? Jim, what happened?"

"It's the vet. Michael is dead."

Rebecca, Jim and I drove in silence.

"I'm sorry, he went into shock at about 3AM, I operated and found a puncture in his lung. It couldn't be seen on x-ray. It was too late, had I done it sooner he might have made it."

The vet handed us a stiff Michael wrapped in clear plastic. Upon our return we dug a hole. Rebecca went to her room and brought back a comb.

"I want Michael to take something of mine with him."

We then dropped Rebecca off at a friends' house, met with a couple from Croton who were to be our witnesses, and in a state of shock I married Jim at the mayor's office. When we arrive home he went off to play tennis with a friend and I went to bed to mourn Michael.

This was not the first time I denied the power of the gifts. "Burn your sister at the stake, she's a witch" the doctors' words were thrown through the door before his body could be seen. My mother and my sister's husband heard that statement and knew my sister had given birth at 2:54PM Tuesday to a 7lb. 11oz blond haired boy. They knew because I had told them what would happen before my sister's last doctors appointment. She had told the doctor and he had laughed and said my prediction was highly improbable, until he came through the delivery door. Hearing their laughter when my mother and my brother-in-law repeated the doctor's words, left me feeling stranger and more alone than ever. The odd looks and silent stares kept alive my determination to shut my mouth in the future. I was sixteen at the time and my silent periods at home were stretching into months.

It was 30 years later that I learned that my sister was offered drugs to ease the pain during labor, looked at a clock that showed the time at 2:30PM and, believing I was right, told the nurse she wouldn't need them. In all those years growing up there were no encounters with people who assisted me in understanding the gift. Yet I know today many who have incredible gifts of prophecy. That is probably why in metaphysics the statement "when the student is ready the teacher appears" is a key. Each of us is student and teacher at varying moments. How could I blame them for what none of us understood?

The one place I remember that kept me feeling at home in a strange, cold environment, was when the "knowing" would take over. It would totally immerse me. One day a woman came to visit. I could "see" a baby growing in her. Not only see it, but feel its sensation at being in a warm, fluid environment. I could feel emotions that were not familiar and at the edges of understanding would come concepts and ideas that would float in me without having a place to land or words to express these experiences for years. Today I say I gestalt (take in the whole experience) the person/plant/animal/proton/insect/universe...etc. Understanding now comes like a bolt of lightning, strong and forceful, all at once. Sometimes the information is completely developed with full sensory input...a vision with words, thoughts, feelings, texture, and odors. It can take me quite a while to sort out the full details and bring it to earth light, practical and detailed. As a child I took the loudest external message...my unique qualities were unacceptable, therefore I was unacceptable. Despite the great messages given to me and the beautiful voice that taught me, my conclusion was that my strangeness...my powers, were a curse to be avoided at all costs. The problem was how to turn away from myself. Gradually over the years I simply stopped believing in the intuitive process. When the visions would come they would break through at a speed I could not stop. Consequently most of the visions became frightening, not only their intensity, but the only ones that could rip through my armor were the most painful of occurrences. The conflict between knowing and refusing to know created a great deal of stress. So much that I had little energy left to make clear decisions or wise moves in my life. Financially I never had more than enough to get by, vacations were always in the future to be dreamed of, I would work until I dropped and feeling guilty and shamed if I was not always kind and good to everyone. Where was I? Hiding, of course. It's funny, I realized many years after the fact, that the things I was hiding were the blessings, the gifts I was dearly protecting from harm. No one was ever going to bruise this precious life again, not if I could prevent it. Of course in believing that I left myself wide open for one trauma after another.

As years of meditating and tuning in to the inner world led me to work with more people and animals in all sorts of situations, I established a trust in the gifts bestowed on me. No longer in conflict, accepting what I had and sharing it led to many strange encounters. Always looking to make up for the pain in my animal friends' lives that I felt partially responsible for, I began to work with people who rescued, ran shelters and adopted all sorts of bruised and battered animal friends.

Reprinted with permission from Grit
Courtesy of Stella Hart/Anne Cousineau

GRIT, MARCH 21, 1982

CHAPTER FIVE
CAN SHE TALK
WITH THE ANIMALS?

Marianne Hatt, is a journalist, Society For the Prevention of Cruely to Animals agent, and horse owner and animal lover. She recounts her early experiences with Nancy:

The way I first became aware of Nancy was through our mutual friend, Sue, in the early 1980's. I was on her animal welfare board, Alibi Acres. The three of us, Nancy, Sue and I had all been working with horses in one way or another. At the time I was writing for a statewide horse publication as a reporter. I called Nancy originally because I wanted to interview her for the New Jersey Horseman. I wanted the interview to be from the animal's point of view, which I hoped Nancy could provide, since she was a psychic known for her animal communications. This was not a popular idea at the time, but I was intrigued by the possibilities. I had also had weird experiences in the past hearing my animals talk to me.

A friendship developed between Nancy and myself and over time she "read" quite a few of my horses. The one I was most impressed with was "Lad." This is the one I used for the interview. I was fascinated by what she had to say. I bought Lad knowing that he had been badly abused. I just had some kind of affinity with this horse where I could hear him practically talking in my head. I had conversations with him all the time and knew what he was going to do before he did it. He was spectacular in the showring. He absolutely hated men because it had been men who had badly abused him. The poor animal was 200 pounds underweight when I bought him. He was a mess.

I had only had Lad a year or so when Nancy read him. He had been doing very well with me and loved being in the showring. He loved the attention. I brought him out to Nancy and they looked at each other. They had quite a mental conversation at that point. Nancy said he was the only horse she had ever read where his third eye did not have to translate. They just had the conversation in plain English. Nancy said his "voice" sounded like a very deep four year old. What struck me in particular was that Nancy said Lad would live to be twenty-eight to thirty years old. He is currently twenty-one and in excellent health. I could put him in the show ring tomorrow if I wanted to. She also told me he would continue to do very well at the shows, and he did indeed go on to win every award there was to win. Another piece of information Nancy got was Lad telling her about a piece of broken cartilage on the end of his nose. This had been broken when his previous owners had twisted it while abusing him. I did not know this at the time, and later had a vet check it and he confirmed that it had been broken. It was so far up in his nose, that without knowing it was there you would never have thought to look for it.

Interestingly, a few years later Lad ended up competing against a horse at a show. The horse belonged to the man whom I had bought him from, and had been his abuser. I told Lad, "You know what you're going to do? You're going to beat that S.O.B." Sure as shooting, he did beat him in the showring.

Another animal Nancy read for me was my cat, Maniac. He was a Himalayan longhair, and at the time was the biggest slob that ever walked. He would not keep himself clean and he hated to be bathed. He had a coat that looked like "who did it and ran." Nancy said to me, "Someday you are going to show that cat." Until that time I had only shown horses and had never dreamed of showing cats. Maniac was twelve years old in August, he is a Double Supreme National Household Pet, and went into the showring for the first time at nine years of age. Today he grooms himself impeccably and is very proud of his appearance. I simply did not believe Nancy at the time.

I used to be an SPCA agent in Morris County in the early 1980's, and Nancy had volunteered to help us on several cases. What we were dealing with were extreme cases of animal cruelty such as ritual killings and cockfights.

The neighbors of a family that had two great danes complained that the dogs had disappeared, but their collars and chains were still there. They were accusing the family of killing their dogs. Nancy told me their son did it, and they were buried in the back yard in plastic bags. She warned me to watch out for him when I went there, as he was very disturbed and dangerous. She said the mother would answer the door, but the son would be listening from a flight of stairs. I took her advice and went in with a police officer.

When we arrived at the house the mother answered the door. Just as Nancy had predicted, the son was listening from a flight of stairs, and he was holding a shotgun. We called in some more armed police officers and then went in. We found the dogs buried in plastic bags in the yard just as Nancy had seen.

The mother knew her son had shot the dogs, but did not report it because she was afraid of him, with good reason apparently. We prosecuted, and in the end the court ordered psychiatric help for the boy. The probable cause for the boy's behavior, it was found, was severe child abuse by his father early in life.

On a more personal level, I have taken what I have learned from Nancy and applied it to my daily life. I have found that my first impressions are rarely wrong and I believe myself. Also, I have learned to explore the inner self. These things, I feel, are very important for everyone.

THE SUN, Thursday, October 21, 1982

Bunny is OK
Stolen dog found in W.Va.

By Gail A. Campbell
Howard County Bureau of The Sun

The call came at 5 p.m. yesterday. Before he could hang up the telephone, James (Duffy) Parthemos was in tears.

Bunny was coming home.

After more than two weeks of advertising in five Maryland newspapers, contacting three psychics, calling every animal shelter in the state, giving out more than 1,000 flyers with the dog's description, and hiring taxis to take his wife around Howard and Baltimore counties searching for the stolen German shepherd, Mr. Parthemos was able to tell his wife her "baby" was safe.

The ads had even carried the words, "Child grieving," a line the childless couple added because they thought it would encourage empathy.

"I fell to my knees in the yard, and I thanked God when he told me," a beaming Susan Parthemos said last night.

Hugging the dirty, sticky, somewhat weary 12-year-old dog to her, she said the reunion was unbelievable.

"When [Gus [her brother] first brought her here, I just hugged and kissed her] It was like a dream," she said, shaking her head.

Through tears and a choked voice, Mr. Parthemos kept saying, "Thank the Lord. I haven't cried so much since my mother died."

Mrs. Parthemos's brother, Gus Malas, retrieved Bunny yesterday after an hour-long search through some woods at Harpers Ferry, W.Va., with two men who wanted the $500 reward offered for the dog's return.

The dog was stolen more than two weeks ago when Mrs. Parthemos ran into a cleaning establishment in the Village Green shopping center on U.S. 40 in Ellicott City. She left the ignition key in her 1971 gold-colored Chevrolet station wagon. When she

came out, both the car and the dog in it were gone.

Bunny's homecoming was the end of a chain of events that began after an article appeared in The Sun last week, Mrs. Parthemos said.

"A man called me last Wednesday, after reading the story and said he'd found my car registration card on Norris street in Baltimore. I called Gus, and he went to the neighborhood and found my car," she recalled.

Mr. Malas said he found the remains of the station wagon near Calhoun and Ramsay streets in Southwest Baltimore. It had been stripped and abandoned.

Since then, Mr. Malas and Mrs. Parthemos combed the neighborhood for any leads as to where Bunny might have been dropped off.

"Today, I begged some people who knew the guy who took my car to tell me where Bunny was. Finally, one guy said he might know where she was, and he and another guy led Gus to West Virginia," Mrs. Parthemos said yesterday.

Mr. Malas said the "guys," whom he would identify only as "Junior" and "Buddy," met him at Mr. Parthemos's Catonsville restaurant, Duffy's, and led him to Harpers Ferry.

"They didn't know where she was for sure either. They said the guy had just dropped her off there and driven the car back to Baltimore to dump it," Mr. Malas said.

"When we got to a place near the Potomac River, we got out of our cars and started walking through the woods. Finally, we went down this dinky road and came out at what looked like a hobo's camp with bottles and trash strewn everywhere," Mr. Malas said.

"We all kept calling Bunny's name, but found nothing. Finally we came to this house near a road, and the lady there said she had seen a dog running up and down the road looking lost and crying for the last

See BUNNY, C10, Col. 3

Susan Parthemos, with Bunny, says their reunion "was lik

THE SUN, Thursday, October 21, 1982

Stolen dog OK, found in Harpers Ferry

BUNNY, from C1

two weeks. She said she had just fed the dog a couple of hours ago," Mr. Malas said.

The woman's husband, Donald Painter, "came with us to show us where he'd last seen" the dog," Mr. Malas said.

"I found Bunny near a pond sleeping in some weeds. She didn't even answer when I called her, she was so out of it. She didn't recognize me, and she

was shaking badly," Mr. Malas said.

Mr. Malas drove her back to Ellicott City last night. Bunny's hair was matted and sticky and she looked exhausted, but she was in good shape, Mrs. Parthemos said.

As soon as the dog was returned about 6:30 p.m., they took her to a veterinarian who said she had a slight fever.

"She's starting to come back now," Mr. Malas said as Bunny, tail wag-

ging and tongue lolling, sniffed around her velvet chaise lounge in the sun porch she likes and got reacquainted with home.

Mr. Parthemos said his restaurant manager paid the two men who led them to Bunny the $500 reward money and let them go, asking no questions.

"That was the deal," he said. "We promised to pay the reward no questions asked, and we did."

Mrs. Parthemos, grinning widely, said she wanted to thank the hundreds of people who called since her dog first disappeared.

"So many people tried to help me look for her. The psychics were right [in saying Bunny would be returned safely]. The kids in Valley Mede [the Ellicott City subdivision where she lives] were terrific, the cab drivers were wonderful, and if it hadn't been for the story in The Sun, none of this would ever have happened."

THE SUN, OCTOBER 21, 1982

CHAPTER SIX
BUNNY'S MISSING

The woman's voice was spilling frantically through the wire as she implored me to find her dog. Bunny was possibly stolen and she was desperate.

"What is your name?"

"Sue Parthemus. I'm sorry but I'm absolutely desperate. Bunny means everything to me. I can't get around well. It's hard to go looking. I found your name in Grit magazine. You do find missing pets, don't you?"

"Sometimes, I'll do whatever I can to help."

My hand still held the telephone and my feet still touched the floor; something I call my being or essence was no longer in Budd Lake, New Jersey. I was traveling with the winds, but faster than I could be aware of. Seconds ago Sue asked a question and now I'm staring out through the eyes of a beautiful, sweet German Shepherd. She reminded me of the first dog I had as an adult.

It was 1968; I was pregnant and married to a nightmare. We lived in Puerto Rico while my husband did research on brain functions. Two weeks after moving from the Bronx, Gil turned into a raging lunatic. Periodically he would slap or punch me, then on bended knees he would cry and apologize. I learned that if I didn't accept his apology, another beating would follow.

Stranded on a beautiful island, no phone, no car, except when he relented to let me use it, and pregnant with complications was as close to hell as I ever want to get. Whatever mistakes and screw ups I've made, that marriage and subsequent problems more than paid for any karma I've accrued.

It was after one of his insane apologies that we went looking for a dog. When I walked in to the breeders home, a three month old puppy was brought out. Love at first sight is a habit with me, especially with animals. I had been reading Ayn Rand's *Atlas*

Shrugged and Galt was the hero who suffered with a dignity I had never seen. He stirred my soul and I embraced the concepts of "riding the pain." So Galt took a ride to Old San Juan. Mary and her little lamb never had it so good. He didn't need training. We were inseparable from the first. Gil hated his being in our bed so as soon as Gil shut the door behind him to go to work, Galt jumped in and put his head on the empty pillow next to mine. Now Galt and Bunny were joined in my heart. Bunny seemed to have the same depth of devotion and sweetness. I ached for her. I ached for the lack of a Galt in my life.

Suddenly aware of the voice on the other end, I answered:

"The first thing I see is Bunny in Virginia. I see her being taken in a station wagon. There are two men in it. They feel like they just pulled a robbery. She is with a man with a shotgun. He is scuzzy looking. I see him on top of a hill."

"That's impossible. My car was stolen, but she's definitely not in Virginia. I live in Maryland, but I'm not near Virginia, that's quite a run. She can't be there. Please I need your help. Can't you tell me anything else.?"

" You had a station wagon?"

"Yes."

" Then I do see it. It's the first town over the border, going directly south from you. I can only tell you what I see. Bunny is a large German Shepherd isn't she?"

"Yes, that's true."

"Then it's her I'm seeing. Call me back when you get any lead or just to talk, I'll see if more comes."

The call came the next day. Breathless with anxiety Sue began:

"Bunny was seen in a station wagon heading south after a robbery with two men driving. The police think they were heading towards Virginia. How did you know? When will they find her? Is she okay?"

"Yes, Bunny is not hurt, but she'll be hungry and scared. I don't see the men harming her."

"How can you be sure?"

"I'm traveling there with my mind, that's how I can tell. Sue, I've been like this ever since I can remember. I'm so glad Bunny has you. You must love each other very much. Thanks for calling and keeping me informed. I'll be praying for her. Keep sending her loving thoughts. Keep your fears away from your thoughts of her. It's important. She's very telepathic, and loving you, she is very sensitive to your thoughts."

"But how am I ever going to get her back? Where is she? She can't be in Virginia?"

"Why don't you send me a photo of her. In the meantime until I get it, please work on letting some of the fear abate and remaining open to the possibilities I'm seeing. I could be wrong I know, but I could also be right. Call me in a day or two."

The photos were on my desk two days later when her call came.

"Hi Sue, okay, this time I see her by railroad tracks. Wait a minute, I think I feel a name coming...Harpers Ferry, West Virginia. Isn't that a movie or something?"

"Are you sure?"

"Yes, hold on there are more images coming. I'm waiting for them to clear."

The images were barely there. Like looking through a long tunnel to see a speck of something. Only you know the speck is the key to a mystery and its important to get a detail shot and somehow enlarge it, translate into common sense and be right.

"There are mountains and water nearby. She's on a mountain, alone. She's waiting for you. You can find her. Sue you are going to see a truck, wooden sides, color green, and there's a bandanna on the seat."

"Is that where Bunny is?"

"No, but it's a clue to tell you that you are on the right track. I think she is by the railroad tracks near the mountain. Poor girl, she misses you. You've been sending her a lot of good messages. I can feel her being comforted."

Sue called back with the good news. Bunny was in her arms again.

I turned to Galt, now many years a spirit: "Thanks for keeping Bunny company, I love you. Just once more I'd love to hug you. You kept me company in some of my darkest moments."
(For Sue Parthemus' comments see Appendix D)

Horses And Psychics: 'They Tell Me Everything'

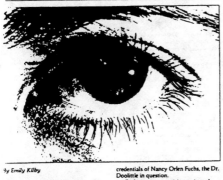

By Emily Kilby

Linda Hepburn wanted to know the reasons behind her new horse's erratic behavior. When she raised the reins to pass them over his head, he plastered his ears to the ceiling. When she attempted to ride him, he took to fits of bucking and shying. His canter gave the impression that he was traveling with one tire flat. Increasingly baffled by her horse's forays into irrational behavior, Hepburn considered a number of actions, from consulting a veterinarian to shipping her horse off to a professional trainer.

Neither idea appealed to her, so she tried something completely different: Hepburn called in a psychic to sit down and have a mental chat with her horse, Amir.

The horse allegedly spilled out his guts to the female Dr. Doolittle, who listened and then translated the conversation from horse to English for the owner. The sad tale was typical: earlier abuse and misunderstanding, inadequate training and pain in the back and one hock had combined to bring the horse to his present state. By the end of the session, Hepburn not only felt she understood her horse better, but had shed her skepticism about the possibility of mental communication between man and animal.

Before assigning this report to your 'there's-a-sucker-born-every-minute" file and putting the notion of talking animals back on the shelf with children's literature where you think it belongs, consider the credentials of Nancy Orlen Fuchs, the Dr. Doolittle in question.

Fuchs is a nonpracticing registered nurse from northern New Jersey. Her psychic powers are reportedly so prodigious that she has located a missing child in faraway Texas, communicated with retarded children and mentally disturbed adults, led SPCA investigators to a backyard burial mound for murdered dogs and aided the police in solving numerous criminal cases. While the police remain hesitant about publicizing their ties with Fuchs, most of her other clients spread the word with a fervor usually found only in religious converts.

Passionate belief is one thing, documentable fact another. Mary Ann Dutton, owner of a title-search agency, writer for the *New Jersey Horseman* and agent for the SPCA, intended to expose a fraud when she invited Fuchs over to "read" her horse. Unlike Hepburn, Dutton knew her horse's history, having acquired him as an abuse case through her humane group work. Dutton's goal was to work up an interesting article for the *Horseman* and, like all good investigative reporters, she planned to paint her subject through questioning into an inescapable corner. Assured that none of their mutual acquaintances had passed on to Fuchs any information about the horse, Dutton began her grilling with questions only she, her veterinarian and her farrier knew the answers to.

According to Dutton, "I sat down on a hay bale and started throwing questions at her:

" 'What's his favorite goodie?'
" 'Sugar-coated doughnuts.'
" 'What's his favorite activity?'
" 'Foxhunting.'
" 'Which kind of riding does he like best?'
" 'Not the kind with the big saddle, the kind with the little saddle, but bigger than the jockeys use.' "

Among Fuchs' predictions and diagnoses were the horse's placings in a show two months later, a broken cartilage in the animal's nose and a description of the man who inflicted the injury with a chain twitch.

Uncovering a potential Fuchs fraud must now pass to some other enterprising *Continued on p. 58*

EQUUS 41/55

Psychics
Continued from p. 55

reporter, since Dutton's skepticism succumbed to the onslaught of the psychic's unerring accuracy. "Nancy has never been wrong in any prediction she's made for me," insists Dutton.

Two people's conversions hardly stand as proof of nonverbal, nonvisible communication between living creatures of different species. Very little disclosed in either of these equine-human encounters would have escaped the notice of an experienced horseman, and that little bit could be ascribed to astute guessing on Fuchs' part. You work with enough horses and people, and you learn how to interpret the subtleties of body language—no mind reading required. The hitch in this rationalization is that Fuchs knows zilch about horses. Born and raised in Brooklyn, she has just recently moved with her family to rural New Jersey because the mental and physical press of the urban masses had grown intolerable. She insists that she has not read up on the subject and claims that she had never so much as touched a horse before her meeting with Hepburn.

Her ignorance of even the most common stable equipment leaves her groping for words when interpreting the horse's thoughts for his owner. "I saw an instrument," she says when recalling one incident, "and the horse started to rear." What kind of instrument? "It has sharp points. A pitchfork." A convincing vagueness, and a possibly convenient one as well. Imagine the horse owner titillated by visions of past cruelties, eagerly supplying the specifics for the obviously sympathetic but grossly ignorant reader. Examined in this light, it's hard to say who has been "read," the horse or the owner.

Still, enough mystery exists in the relationship between man and animal to feed legends of men like John Rarey and The Whisperer who supposedly hypnotized equine lions and had them behaving like lambs within a few hours. And what about the "natural" horsemen among us whose way with horses can't be precisely defined and imparted to others? Henry Blake, a "natural" himself, wrote up his explanations in a book, *Talking With Horses*. After years of experimentation, Blake is convinced that extrasensory perception and mental telepathy serve as conduits for communication between man and animal and that the ability is not restricted to a select few. Receptivity is the key.

Psychics say they "tune in" or "open up" to the "energy fields" emitted by every living creature—which leads to a major stumbling block to acceptance of

EQUUS CONTINUED

psychic phenomena. These image merchants, perhaps afflicted by an occupational dysfunction of sorts, are lost for words when asked to explain the process: "It's a feeling of opening up to the subject, of being one with the subject," explains a Virginia psychic who converted to the belief 10 years ago. "It's like you become the subject." Far out, as they used to say.

Those willing to accept the jargon and take the leap out of the rational "seeing is believing" world into the intuitive realm of the mind come back with some interesting observations. Tricia Douglas, who reads horses as part of her "holistic health program" at the Balanced Equitation Center in Santa Barbara,

California, has found that "the unhappiest horses are the ones under the greatest pressure to perform—the show horses and racehorses. They're kept inside all the time under the most unnatural conditions. The happiest horses are the ones kept in the most natural conditions possible. There's really a strong tie between the emotions of the horse and his physical condition." The Virginia psychic cited earlier claims that horses are particularly responsive to eye contact with their human companions, even though scientific evidence would indicate that the animal's close-up vision is so poor as to block any such communication. Fuchs further suggests that an owner can improve his horse's performance in competition by

beaming mental images of the particulars of the contest into his brain for several days before the event.

If you're willing to take the leap yourself and spend a little extra time inside your horse's brain, the least you will have done is lavish additional attention on your animal. But one thing is for sure. If you're considering calling in a psychic to unlock the mysteries of your horse's mind, you'd better not have any skeletons—horse or human—you want kept hidden in the tack room. For, according to Fuchs, "horses have complete memory of everything that happens to them from birth. They tell me everything." ∎

Reprinted with permission from Equus Magazine

EQUUS CONTINUED

CHAPTER SEVEN
HALLUCINATIONS OR VISIONS?

In September of 1975 I entered a strange new world. It was three months after visiting another psychic in Brooklyn. Jim had taken me for my first psychic reading. What an experience, it left me feeling like I had gone to the strangest place in my head and yet it was so familiar I felt like I finally came home. I will always thank Jim in my heart and prayers for the change he helped bring about.

Three months later I was ready for more. I read an ad for a lecture by a psychic healer. It was being given in the basement of a bank a mile down the road from my house in Peekskill, New York. Terrified of hanging out with a bunch of weird people who believed in this "stuff" I called the number given. After a reassuring conversation with a woman named Fran, I hung up thinking it was more like going to the movies, you don't have to be involved if you don't want to.

Sunday evening I parked my car in the bank parking lot and joined a crowd of people heading toward the doors. A woman sat by the door collecting the donation of $3. I paid and started walking into a room set up with about 200 seats. A man turned to me and introduced himself.

"Hi, I'm Alan Pregno, care to sit with me."

"Sure...... Pregno, I've heard that name before. I know, that's the name of my title insurance company."

"That's my brother. I work for him. What house did you buy?"

"The white one on Wooddale Ave. in Peekskill."

"Sure I know it, I did the work on it."

"Why are you here?"

"I study astrology primarily, but am curious about all of it."

We sat in our new friendship happily exchanging smiles when the speaker was introduced. Nancy Pisano walked up to the podium and my eyes froze. I was seeing a hallucination, only this time everyone saw her.

Back in June the fourth of 1969 I spent 48 hours in labor, mostly due to neglect. Two weeks after delivering my daughter I was critically ill. I weighed 145 lbs at 5'8" tall after I delivered Rebecca. I was brought into the hospital again on June 18th weighing 103 lbs. When I came out of the hospital for the second time my mother and Gil were not talking. I remember walking into my daughter's room and seeing my mother angrily diapering Rebecca. This tiny creature was in mother's keeping. My mother had a safety pin in her hand and she was emphasizing her words by pointing the open pin towards me. Somehow I was to blame for Gil's behavior towards her. By nightfall the two so-called adults were screaming at each other. I grabbed my daughter out of her crib, she was now wide awake and crying, and ran upstairs to my friends and neighbors, Bob and Sharon.

"Get those lunatics out of my home, please."

I think they were more shocked at my outburst than at the situation. Gil screaming was not unusual, but my call for help was. I don't remember how the evening passed but it did. The next morning my father arrived from New York. Taking his wife away from that hellhole, he accused me of being the cause of the problem. Somewhere in a corner of my heart all hope was lost. I sunk into a deep depression, believing Rebecca and my fate were now in the hands of a Jekyl and Hyde.

A few days later a visitor appeared. I remember the first time I saw her. She was sitting on the edge of my bed. I didn't know her name and when I asked she didn't seem to respond. She was a pretty caucasian woman with black hair, big blue eyes and a soft featured face. The prettiest thing about her was the color of her clothes. They were bright royal blue. Everytime I saw her she wore her blue suit, along with a blue pillbox hat.

As sick as I was, I figured I was now crazy. Part of me decided that since I was already out of my mind I may as well enjoy the excursion so I asked her what she wanted.

"Go into the waters."

Into the waters? She's crazy. If I were to go across the street to the cliffs and jump into the water I would die. We lived in Old San Juan on Boulevard Del Valle. We were directly across the street from an old fort that was high up above the port to Puerto Rico.

She didn't seem vicious so I figured she couldn't have meant what it sounded like. The words seemed to enter my heart and offer peace. What waters could she mean? I didn't look further for an answer. It was so reassuring to receive comfort and friendship, a feeling that someone cared, that I was fearful of investigating too closely. I didn't want her to disappear. I was so happy to hear loving thoughts that I didn't care that it came from a hallucination, so the next visit to one of my physicians I spoke to him about it. His response was quite fascinating considering he was my gastro-enterologist.

"I don't know what it is, but she certainly doesn't sound like a hallucination."

"Why not?"

"Because you can talk about it and distinguish her from me and you."

"Then what is she and why does she insist I go into the waters? Am I suicidal?"

"It doesn't sound like that. All I can suggest is what she isn't. I have no idea what she is. You may be ill and you may be depressed but going into the water doesn't sound like a suicidal thought to me. Maybe it's symbolic."

I left his office hoping he was right. When I saw her again I asked if she was a hallucination.

"You may call me anything you wish," said the new voice in my head.

A few days later she disappeared as soft as a puffy cloud on a breezy day. It wasn't until Nancy Pisano got up to talk that I understood who and what that vision was. There she was, and what was she talking about?

"The spiritual waters..." her voice continued.

Of course, the spiritual waters. Nancy must have spirit traveled to me, a call for help was answered by a loving and devoted healer. The decision to attend her Monday night psychic development classes in Newburgh, New York was less frightening than the decision to walk into the basement of the bank. Chipping away at my fear of the hidden world of metaphysics became more of a game.

A week later Nancy gave me my second reading.

"You will be a teacher in the field within the year."

My emotions danced with excitement at her words while my heart raced with fear. Conflict was becoming my closest companion with each step I took. Well, I couldn't be a teacher without my own permission. I comforted my fears promising not to do anything that would leave me in a panic. I forgot that when you throw yourself into something, you look up later and notice what you have done. I could always work well in a crisis and to me, this new field had definite symptoms of a crisis in my view of reality.

Alan became a close friend. In the evenings I would practice by giving him and anyone he brought with him a reading. It was a strange time, everything was new and I kept walking into the darkest corners of my mind. Soon a little light began to be a steady beam shining on these weird spaces I would go to.

Thursday night, sometime in 1976. It was almost a year later when I began teaching a meditation, psychic/spiritual development class. A dozen or so regular clients had suggested that I gather them together on a regular basis. Another prediction had come true.

It was one of those Thursdays' that Nancy O'Connor, student, client, and friend rushed into class late and breathless.

Nancy has a face shaped by kindness and loss. A sweet sad look usually sat in her eyes, but tonight there was troubled concern.

"Sorry, I'm late but one of my horses has a problem and I didn't want to leave the kids with it. I left Jane, the groom there anyhow, to see if she could calm him down."

A vision popped up in my third eye.

"Nancy, I see something. Let me show you on paper. I don't know the anatomy of a horse well enough to name the parts I'm seeing."

Grabbing paper and pen I drew a rough outline of a horse. On the lower part of the back and to the right I put an X.

"This area is injured."

"I can call over to the barn and check on it. Can I use your phone?"

"Jane, go over to Fellow and touch him and tell me what happens."

Success..."Now what do we do? She touched him where you said and he jumped."

"Have her get some Olive Oil, slightly warm it and gently rub it over that area. Then take the ends of the muscles and firmly pull them in opposite directions. Lastly, tell her to keep that area warm and when she is finished to place her palms down on the spot and imagine pouring light down from the universe, through her body, through her palms and into Fellow. While she is doing that she can mentally send him a message of love and help, telling him to use the energy to help alleviate his suffering."

All made up, I had no idea what I was talking about, just kept following an image I was seeing and words I was hearing. "Imagination is the act of imaging. What is made up? Where does it come from? Who really knows? Not me, it's all made up. I figure I'll know for sure sometime after I leave my body permanently and then it may not matter."

The next week Nancy came in on time.

"Thank you Nancy. Fellow is back to his old wonderful self. Jane did exactly as you said and by the time she was finished, she could feel him relax as if he knew she was helping. Saved us a vet bill, too. Anytime you want a ride just let me know."

I've never taken Nancy or anyone up on that offer. Don't even know why, except that my spinal injuries are extensive enough that I no longer attempt to do things I sense would lead my body into more difficulties. In my early days of attempting to recover I would go out dancing for hours, just to release the emotional turmoil and escape the pain. Of course the next day it would be worse. Amazing how slow a learner I was. It took years to stop insisting on doing things that would no longer add up as a huge payment for fun.

Horses and I relate well as long as I am sending them healing and love. I always think they know I wish for them an existence where they are treated as if they have a soul, not as a commodity. Some of the folks I have met know the difference and have a lot of respect for their animal friends, while others treat them as if they are chattel, just as women, children, orientals, blacks, jews, and any-one standing out as weaker have been bought and sold at various times in our evolutionary process.

(For Nancy O'Connor's story of working with Nancy and attending her weekly psychic class, see Appendix E)

Friday, June 15, 1984

41

HORSE CARE

PSYCHIC AT WORK

Linda S. Hepburn

The chestnut stallion half-reared and struck out with a slender foreleg when the dark-haired woman reached out to touch his neck. She jumped back and two grooms quickly closed in to restrain him.

"See what I mean?" prompted the owner from outside the stall. "He put one of my men in the hospital, quiet one minute, flies off the wall the next!"

The woman approached again, speaking quietly, and the stallion allowed her to stroke his back. As she slowly worked her way up his withers, neck and jaw, he stuck his head out in front of him, moving his lips and occasionally clacked his teeth together.

Without even looking into the horse's mouth, she said, "His teeth are done wrong. He's got a toothache, and he's so bright, he's trying to show you. His vagus nerve is inflamed, his sinuses are under pressure and he's trying to relieve it. When his pain is lowered, he's a love. But when he's in pain, he's like anybody else."

Curious stable hands paused to watch as the bluejean-clad, 29-year-old Nancy Fuchs of Morris County, New Jersey, stood face to face with the barn's most volatile stallion and made bold medical conclusions without aid of X-ray, stethoscope or lab tests.

Knowing that veterinarians have struggled with veterinary school, the latest surgical techniques and sometimes uncooperative horses, one might find the preceding scenario hard to believe. Finding a toothache and nerve inflammation without even opening the horse's mouth is quite unusual.

Yet, Nancy Orlean Fuchs, psychic healer, has been called upon by dozens of show, racing and backyard stables along the East Coast to "diagnose" equine ailments ranging from dietary problems to bad jumping form. While not all her clients like to publicize their ties with Fuchs, others happily share news of their first encounter with psychic healing.

Her clients claim she can detect food allergies too minute to be measured by scientific instruments, physical reasons for behavioral problems, energy imbalances from long-forgotten injuries, and that special winning presence called "heart." While her unorthodox methods don't sit well with the majority of the veterinary establishment, some veterinarians are good-naturedly moving over to make room for some "second guessing."

Veterinarian Dr. David Jefferson witnessed Fuchs pinpoint the site of an old injury on a horse who had long since healed, showed no scar, and was no longer limping. Fuchs claimed the animal still felt pain in that region.

When Dr. Jefferson tested Fuchs by holding Butazolidin in one closed fist, and Methenamine (kidney pills) in the other, Fuchs consistently "guessed" which hand held the medicine that would alleviate the lameness pain.

Whether she was actually sensing the chemistry of the hidden pills, reading the veterinarian's mind, or making several lucky guesses was not the question. The horse had been operated on successfully and had recovered, making rediscovering the old injury site seem useless.

However, Fuchs believes, old injuries can cause problems for the horse. By compensating for the weakened area, he may overstress another seemingly unrelated muscle or organ. Over time, the living system loses its delicate balance as the body makes small sacrifices in order to allow the horse to carry on with its work.

Energy flow, on which all living systems depend, may become rerouted from its normal path, or even blocked, with no nutrients getting to the blocked area. Fuchs teaches owners how to "move" the energy with their hands and push it past the "roadblock" or put it back on its normal path.

Unless you are an applied kinesiologist (one who studies mechanics and anatomy in relation to movement), this intuitive approach to healing might leave you looking for the phone number of your trusted veterinarian. Countless horses have been healed by rest and conventional medicine and gone on to great competitive achievements. For a vet, Fuchs' approach can appear to be a no-win situation.

Dr. Jefferson is one veterinarian who has decided to take it all in stride. "I had serious doubts about her at first. I can see why she might raise some questions in an owner's mind. But it's no worse than finding out your clients are reading horse health care publication on the side. If they're learning new things, they're naturally going to have more questions," he said.

Some would argue that despite the controversy surrounding any new equine health treatment, there's always room for a second opinion. After all, the horse is the ultimate benefactor of the owner's quest for knowledge. Even if the energy rerouting had no effect whatsoever, perhaps the horse can sense that we are rooting for him, and respond to us mentally, if not physically.

Still, one wonders if psychics, who speak in terms such as "auras," "energy paths" and "imaging," are merely preying on people's feelings for their animals.

Nancy Fuchs, busy raising two children and administering to her human clientele, smiles and shrugs. "I'm only trying to help. I'm not asking everybody to do things my way or to believe the things I believe."

Using her police work as an example, she explains, "I don't call them on the phone when I get a revelation or a clue to a case they're working on. They get enough people calling in, offering helpful advice. But by the time they have exhausted all avenues and not solved the mystery, they are ready to try anything. They come to me simply because every rational approach has failed.

"It's the same with the horses. If the owner has tried the conventional medicine, therapy, training or whatever, and the horse isn't responding, I might be called in. The fact that I am able to help many of these cases disturbs those who aren't ready to tune in to the horse at that level."

Mrs. Sherlock Gillet of Parkton, Maryland, was rerouting energy on a daily basis with one of her event horses. She notes that he hated it at first, always pinning his ears or turning his head away. After several weeks of moving the energy from his rump toward his head, Gillet went out to the barn one day to find the horse standing and staring in a corner of his stall. Since he usually greeted her with much exuberance, she was alarmed at his withdrawn attitude.

"He wasn't eating, but he wasn't sick," she recalls. "We didn't ride him, but we didn't feel it was necessary to call the vet. Nancy Fuchs called us later that day from New Jersey and said, 'Don't be surprised if he goes through this crisis period, because his energy is reversing.' I was concerned, of course, but he came around perfectly normal. In fact, he seems more peaceful and contented. I think he's happier about our sessions as well, and his jumping form has improved."

Reprinted with permission of The Chronicle Of The Horse

THE CHRONICLE OF THE HORSE
JUNE 15, 1984

Page Eight   MT. OLIVE CHRONICLE, THURSDAY, JULY 31, 1980

Local Psychic Reads Amir, Tells Of Years Of Neglect

WASHINGTON TWP. — Arising from the myths of goblins and witches, psychics are gaining more credibility in society.

It is not uncommon, for example, to see a psychic predicting the future along with a newscast of current events.

Linda Hepburn of Long Valley recently sought out the help of the psychic Nancy Fuchs of Budd Lake to explain the odd behavior and history of her horse, Amir.

A bit skeptical at first, Hepburn was impressed with the results.

During her visit, Fuchs related the time that Amir bucked-off a friend of Hepburn's. Hepburn couldn't understand the horse's behavior, because the friend had ridden him before without trouble.

Fuchs believed the horse had been poked in the side, and Hepburn remembered she had put a new saddle on Amir that day that was stiff and could have rubbed the horse's side.

The psychic said the horse is between 16 and 18 years old, information which could be verified by checking the horse's teeth.

Information Fuchs gave about the horse's history can not be easily verified. She said the horse was born in upstate New York and that he was mistreated during his lifetime.

According to Fuchs, the horse favors Hepburn because "nobody was ever concerned about him before."

Fuchs claims she communicates telepathically with animals. She said she mentally asks the animal a question and the response is "spoken in her head."

She said the same process occurs when a psychic communicates telepathically with someone who speaks a foreign language.

The brain translates the thought into English.

'Finds' People

Although she communicates telepathically with animals, and has helped people locate lost pets, most of Fuchs' work is with people.

Hundreds of people have come to her for advice and instruction. She has taught classes at psychotherapy centers throughout the area, and has conducted workshops for such organizations as the Association for Humanistic Psychology at Princeton University.

She helps people control and develop their psychic abilities and to tune-in the source of insight, comfort and inspiration ,she believes exists below the surface of the mind.

She gives personal readings and many of her clients are referred by

Reprinted with permission from The Mount Olive Chronicle

THE MOUNT OLIVE CHRONICLE
JULY 31, 1988

doctors, psychiatrists and psychologists.

One man, referred to Fuchs by a psychiatrist, had a memory block. Fuchs "saw" the man as a child being driven to a home for boys, where he was cornered and assaulted in a bathroom.

The man looked terrified, Fuchs said, but he finally remembered the incident. His mother was taken ill when he was seven, and he was taken to an orphanage for two weeks. The memory was so painful that he had blocked it and had psychological problems ever since.

Fuchs said she has also helped people with physical problems. She works with a chiropractor, who checks a person physically, while she reads them psychically. She said they try to line up the emotional and physical levels.

Recalls Incident

One person who came to Fuchs for help had epilepsy. Fuchs told him that he had been hit on the head by a baseball when he was 12, and his physical problems started after that incident.

The person remembered the baseball accident, but had not connected it with his epilepsy. His doctors then worked on relieving cranium pressure, and she said his condition improved.

Fuchs said she has also communicated with people who have "passed over."

She worked with the two young owners of a corporation after their father died. The two people were at a loss because they did not know many of the details of the corporation.

Fuchs contacted the former owner several times and helped the young people settle the details.

There are two explanations for communicating with someone who has passed over, according to Fuchs. One thought is that the psychic is actually reading the mind of someone who was close to the deceased; the other explanation is that the psychic is actually communicating with the deceased.

Fuchs believes the second explanation.

She has also made investment predictions. A year and a half ago, Fuchs predicted that gold would rise in price to $437, and then almost double.

"Everyone thought I was crazy — including me," Fuchs said. She didn't invest in the gold.

Fuchs admits her readings and predictions are sometimes wrong,

although errors don't happen frequently.

People are psychics because they are generally accurate in their predictions," she said.

How does Fuchs find the answers for the people who seek out her help?

She psychically becomes the other person for a moment — and then she has all of the answers. She believes people hold the answers within themselves, and have to dig them out.

Fuchs has also worked with police departments to help them track down criminals. She helped police in Connecticut find the person responsible in a multiple rape case.

Childhood Experiences

She has had psychic experiences since she was a child — her family called her a witch. But her ability disappeared when she was 17, and shortly afterwards she suffered a severe back accident.

Fuchs was working as a psychiatric nurse, when a 300-pound patient

fell on her. Twelve years of pain and 34 hospital stays followed that accident.

In desperation, Fuchs husband, Paul, took her to a psychic. The psychic told her she was a healer, and that a psychic channel was blocked in her causing the pain.

The psychic told Fuchs to go home and heal herself. She went home, put her hands on her back, and the pain went away.

"That release from the pain was a gift of spirit or of God to tell my being a psychic was real — that was the turning point of my life," she said.

The psychic also warned her if she shut down her psychic channels again, the pain would return.

She has worked to develop her powers over the past four years.

Fuchs has two children, Becky, 11, and Jessie, nearly 6, and they both share their mother's ability.

Most children have psychic abilities, she said, but most parents teach children to ignore it and to shut it off.

Reprinted with permission from The Mount Olive Chronicle

THE MOUNT OLIVE CHRONICLE CON'T.

CHAPTER EIGHT
FIRST TOUCH

In the same year a woman named Linda called. From the moment I heard her sweet, open, direct, and caring voice. I couldn't wait to meet her.

"I read an article about your work. I have a horse that I need help with, would you please come see him?"

"Sure. What day?"

The day was the following Monday. Linda lived in what is commonly called God's Country. Acres of flat land, flowers by the side of the road, horses grazing everywhere. Looking past the barns and homes the land rose like a tidal wave, only this was covered with froth made of trees and stone. The mountains were red and gold with touches of green.

A woman who looked like a gazelle with long straight light brown hair was standing in the driveway. She had stepped out of a back door when my car pulled up. Linda had a grace about her like she was flying free across the land.

"Nancy?"

"Hi Linda."

"Would you mind if another person watched besides me?"

"Not at all."

She went in to only to return a moment later with a man carrying a camera.

"Hi, I'm Robert. I work at the local paper. Linda called and told me you were coming out here. Would you mind if I report on what I observe?"

"Not at all."

I followed Linda to the barn.

"Remember, I don't want to know anything about the horse, except perhaps its name. I like to call everybody by their name."

"Midnight."

"Thanks."

We walked into the barn. A horse called out. Linda walked over to a stall:

"Midnight, this is the lady I called to help." Her hand was stroking his face.

Linda put a rope on him with a very short lead.

"Would you mind leading him out to the field with Robert? I have to check something."

Not bothering to tell Linda I had never been near a horse, I said:

"Sure," as I took the lead and started chatting with Midnight and Robert as we walked.

"Midnight, whatever is wrong, just let me know and I'll try to help."

We stood in the middle of a field scattered with bright colors. Never having learned the name of most flowers, all I could spot were the daisies. The blue flowers were like stars that dropped from sky, pink ones looked like delicate air brushed fluff and yellow ones looked like pieces of the sun's rays. It was beautiful and helped me center my mind on Midnight.

Connecting with him was easy, I soon found a feeling that translated as a history of trauma. My body seemed to change into a horse's, except that I was the only one who knew that. My front shoulder ached, my head had old damage from a fall as a baby. I could see me as a young colt falling backwards. Then the image changed to one where all my insides grew sluggish and tired. I knew that feeling well, I label that one allergies.

Translating my experience to Linda and Robert was easy. I simply deleted the part where I became an animal. We kinetically muscle tested Midnight for those substances he ingested. I used Linda as a proxy. Two products seemed to show a weakening in the system. Linda decided to switch to other feed and see if that would help.

"I want us to win in the shows, I know he is good enough."

"Linda, he gets nervous when he doesn't know what's coming. Not unlike many of us, he handles change poorly. If you can go to the place where the show is being held beforehand and firmly fix an image of it in your mind it would help. Take that image and stand before him, imagine making mental contact, third eye to third eye and send the image again and again along an imaginary beam."

At the conclusion Linda again handed me the rope. Casually I took it and pulled Midnight along. When he resisted I tugged laughing, "Stubborn as any man I've ever met." I kept on pulling and teasing until I turned the rope back to Linda and started to breathe again. Glad that he was fun and I could handle him I said,

"He was an absolute joy to work with."

"Yes, he was quite different today, thank God. Usually he kicks and bites, that was one of the reasons I called you. Funny how good he was, you sure do know horses."

Back in the comfort of my car my mind shook harder than my body at the risk I had just taken. Sometimes I get in trouble and sometimes I don't, but I always like to jump into the world while it's spinning.

Linda called a month later to tell me she did everything I showed her and they won their first prize easily. In the years that followed they consistently won and grew very close as friends.

Many years later Linda and I laughed at my first experience with a horse. Linda invited me to her wedding two years later. When she and her husband later separated, she came to live in my home in Budd Lake. Midnight was moved to a friend's farm. She attended my wedding on February 11, 1989. A month later her sister called to tell me that Linda went mountain climbing for the first time along with her boyfriend, and an expert teacher. Linda fell off the mountain and died. There is so much more I want to see happen for her that never can be and yet I know Linda is handling her world better than her family and friends are handling missing her. As much as I understand and believe in life after life and reincarnation, it doesn't make the loss go away. It does add other ingredients, comfort to know she's okay, mysterious meetings out of body, her voice ringing true and clear in my mind, all these stretch the emotions into acceptance.

※※※

*NANCY (ACCOMPANIED BY SANDY VAN HOOSE AND
MURPHY THE POODLE) AT THE NBC TV STUDIO IN LOS
ANGELES FOR THE TAPING OF "THE OTHER SIDE,"
JANUARY 10TH, 1995*

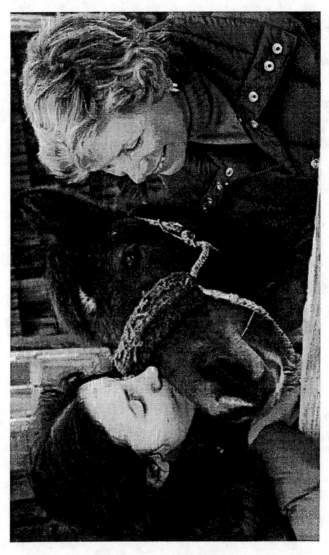

Photo courtesy of Stella Hart & Anne Cousineau

*NANCY WITH "KING NEPTUNE," A MISSING HORSE
SHE FOUND, AND FRIEND, SUE.*

Top Of The Line Farms

33 North Ave. Montvale, N.J. 07656
(201) 930-0506

Mrs. Nancy Weber
27 Bald Nob Road
Denville, New Jersey 07834

Dear Nancy,

We wish to express our gratitude for the wonderful equestrian workshop that you gave at our stable.

Your insight and ability to know each horse, their personality and any physical problem is phenomenal. Many of our boarders followed your advice and had very positive results.

Our personal thanks for your feelings on our daughter's horse, Rae Vin. We followed your advice and his back problems have been totally eliminated. Your prediction for their winning future together proved to be so accurate. Since then they have won many first place awards and championships.

We look forward to another workshop soon, and thank you again for sharing your special gift with us.

Sincerely,

Beverly Van Blarcom
Owner

LETTER FROM TOP OF THE LINE FARMS

CHAPTER NINE
THE HORSE INDUSTRY

By 1984 I had had at least four years of working regularly with animals.

The call was from Jim, a trainer I met through a wonderful couple, Marlene and Galen Sweigart. I had worked with them as individuals and as pony trainers. They are two of the more dedicated and caring animal owners I have ever run across. Galen has gone on to teach many other people healing techniques to use on people and animals, and, when last we spoke, was still thick in the study of healing modalities.

It is a beautiful autumn morning, a perfect day for a long drive into Pennsylvania horse country. The drive makes the day more like a holiday in the country, not work. The roads are lined with blazing fall colors everywhere, in the sky, on the ground and in the process of leaving their temporary homes on the ends of the arms of their parent towards the earth where they rejoin with all. It's an awesome journey and I love watching it happen. The directions are easy, hardly any turns until I get to their town. Two hours of solitude and I am ready for people.

Jim came striding to the car, a walk created from thousands of hours on horses. Long lean muscles, hair that never looks combed. Eyes that showed he had one focus and one focus only...horses. In all the times I spent working with Jim I never got to know him except for his concern for the animals in his care.

"Hi Jim, thanks for the directions they were perfect."

As I pull up, Jim is all questions and nervousness..... "How many people can follow you about? Are the owners permitted to be there? We've got about eleven horses for you to see."

"Jim, as long as everyone can fit in the barn, it doesn't matter to me who or how many people show up. Just please tell everyone not to discuss the animals out loud until I've worked on them."

When I am on an assignment for an animal I ask the owner and trainers not to fill me in on why they called me until I ask. First I need to connect with the animal, soul to soul, establishing a strong bond between us so that the truth of where we each come from is understood by both of us.

They are ready for me. There must be two dozen people, a half dozen dogs and unknown number of cats all curious about the newcomer. A dog runs up to greet me. I love animals, they have a way of making me feel welcome, as if they can still feel the shy little girl present in me.

"Let me introduce you to everyone."

Introductions done, a glass of water in hand, and someone carrying a tape recorder starts us down towards the first stall Jim had chosen for me to enter.

In the stall is a big, beautiful chestnut male with a star on his forehead. He is taller than average and more muscular. the name on the stall reads Flying King.

"Hello," my mind sends. "I'm here to be with you anyway that will help. Please show me what you need. I love you."

My head went reeling with pain. I almost fell over in the grip of shooting, knife like pain that was all over my head. Migraines, my God, how horrible. This horse had gripping waves of head pain that kept him both furious and scared. Tears welled up in me, how could he not be crazy, that poor soul. My hands became charged with my feelings of concern. Every cell of the me I knew and parts I was only vaguely aware of became dedicated to helping him be free of his misery. "God, please bring through me whatever powers of healing and love that will aid in the most loving way possible, this soul who waits for help."

My hands felt warmer than they did a moment ago, my fingers were tingling. Gently I placed my hands on the left side of his back. Moving my hands slowly, I would listen carefully for what they could tell me. Images of a network of energy floated before me. Like a greyish blue gauze that has depth and motion to it, I watched it vibrate beneath my hands. Wherever it showed itself to be twisted or I heard a discordant rhythm to the energy, I would leave my hands over the sight and pray that God's Light would pass through me into my friend.

About a half hour later my hands were massaging and gently pressing the top of his head. His eyes were droopy and relaxed. I could feel a realignment take place in my image of his cranial sutures. My hands walked down to the right jaw, massaging with my fingers, more and more vigorously, then his left jaw. He then rested his head on my shoulder, gently nudging me. "I love you too, you sweetie." We were in complete empathy, mutually open and trusting. Powerful rushes of his love poured through me as we kept the cycle going.

Not moving from our circle of light, I asked, "can I have a brush please?"

A moment later a brush appeared from the crowd. My desire to brush his mane sent shivers down my right arm into my fingertips. As I held the brush I lost all sense of separation. My fingers, the brush and the mane were joined as one. Long strokes stirred with gentle, coaxing words flowed between us. The brush became a bridge of love, a conduit between horse and woman. His eyes followed me with curiosity.

"I'm just brushing your beautiful mane. I hope you're feeling better."

Gradually I looked up and noticed no one had moved. I was so engrossed in our reverie I could not discern their expressions. Only that they looked strange. I wondered what was wrong.

"Anybody care to say something, ask something?"

Jim was the first: "How did you do that?"

"Do what?"

Jim continued, "No one has been able to touch his head since we've had him. All he would do was bite and kick. Couldn't even brush his mane."

"How long is that?"

"Three years."

"I guess if I had the equivalent of a migraine for three years I'd be pretty nasty. Matter of fact, when I have chronic pain there is a particular word most people could use to describe me. It rhymes with witch."

The rest of the day was simple. Flying King had helped me show the people what I do. They were easier to work with after that. I worked on ten more horses, none as troubled as King. Everyone was eager to help their own horse. One woman asked if I would look at a dog, it was having some problems. When people are open to an idea, more creative flow occurs and everything gets easier. Of course there is a danger to that. It all depends on what kind of idea you are working on. Ethics need to get mixed into the recipe.

When we all said good-bye, I ran back to kiss King one more time and to thank him for letting me be a part of his life.

A few days later the trainer called to tell me he could brush the horse's mane for the first time. Weeks later he told me the horse had become increasingly affectionate and easy to work with.

A strange twist occurred when a reporter from a horse magazine called me and wanted references. I gave her a few names to call, among them this horse's owner. The owner refused to speak telling the reporter that she would not want it known that her horse ever had a problem as the price for resale could go down. I always felt sad knowing that it was more important to keep high money value on an animal than to care for them effectively.

※※※ ※※※ ※※※

CHAPTER TEN
DONALD'S PUPPY

Late October, 1988

Sandy Harris had a Doberman Pinscher who was 12 weeks old. She had him because of a friend. Sandy brought this little Doberman back from a Doberman show in California because she knew that her friend Donald was going to die. He had cancer and it was just a matter of time.

Don was Sandy's closest friend and she knew that this was his last time at a dog show. He had seen this little puppy and said, "I just have to have that puppy." They were both professional dog handlers. Sandy hoped that by buying the puppy she would give Don the belief that he would be around in two years, which would be when they would be able to start to show the dog.

Sandy brought the dog home. She lives in the middle of nowhere, isolated. Nearly one thousand acres, surrounded by the Pastiche river. The river suddenly stops its course and goes around, surrounding this acreage, and she lives at the head of the acreage. She had an older female Dobie,who never gets lost, so on a Sunday morning at 9:00 AM Sandy, her dog and the puppy took to the main roads so this little dog would know where he was. Sandy's faithful companion, Astin, who was ten years old, was running ahead with the little puppy following her.

Astin took them on the main trail. Sandy and Astin knew the land very well. When Astin made a right turn, Sandy knew where she would go, and made the right turn off into the field after her. Sandy then saw her make another turn, with the puppy following, but they were quicker, and that was the last Sandy saw of them. She called and called, and finally saw this was useless after an hour and went back to her house. Sandy's husband, Joe said, "Astin's here." Sandy said, "I'm going to kill her, but at least they're back." Then Joe replied, "They're not back. Astin is back." By this time it was about 11:00 AM. Sandy went out to look for the puppy again.

Three hours passed and she still had not found the puppy.

It was winter, it was very cold and this was a very little puppy. He was not used to the cold or being outside. He had no idea where he was, and it was now 3:00 PM. Sandy panicked. She took Astin, and also rounded up quite a few other people with herding dogs and retrievers to help her look. Still no puppy. It was now nighttime.

Sandy was up all night long, calling this dog that didn't even know his name. She barked, howled and pleaded. She thought he might be scared into barking. He probably was scared to death, but he did not answer her barks or howls.

The woods were endless. Sandy kept looking with other dogs. When one got tired she would go back and get a different one. She had experiences with dogs becoming feral after just a few hours of being lost. They become frightened and disoriented, they don't even know you. She thought he would relate better to another dog, so she just kept searching with them. She had visions of the puppy starving and becoming weaker. He had plenty of water because it had been raining, at least.

Sandy called me on a Tuesday night. She had exhausted every other possibility. Then she remembered that a friend of hers knew someone with psychic abilities who had found a lost dog in New York City after the dog had been gone for about six weeks. She called her friend and was given my name and phone number. Sandy was hysterical. I told her that I saw a garage and willow trees. She said, "Willow trees don't grow wild, and I've been all through the woods, hundreds and hundreds of acres. There are only two willow trees and I planted them myself by my barn, which is 500 feet from the house." I continued telling her that I also saw sewers, pipes and ditches. She answered, "There ain't no such thing." I went on to tell her that I also saw a golf course. "Wrong," she said, "You're completely off base." Then I told her to let me think about this overnight and that I would get back to her in the morning. Sandy felt as though her last hope had vanished into thin air.

After we hung up Sandy started thinking. There were no sewers, but the power company came into these woods not that long ago. Maybe ten years ago, and they wanted to put up power lines. There was a river and they couldn't put up the lines. They came also to build a road, and what did they do? They brought these great big sewer pipes and threw them in what Sandy thought was a tributary of a river. They thought they could cover them with dirt and drive their trucks over them. Then Sandy said to herself, "Sewer pipes." She also realized that I had said ditches. Sandy went off to question one of her neighbors. Sandy's neighbor who lives in an old farmhouse (this land was part of a farmstead about 100 years ago) said, "let me explain it to you. When this was a farm, lots of times it went under water, so they had to dig ditches. They dug at least twenty of them. These ditches were dug from the high part to the low part. Then they built a big ditch that went into the river. They are sewer pipes now." What Sandy thought was a river was really a drainage ditch. Now, it's the middle of the night, it's pouring, and out she went to search around the ditches about a half mile from her house. Altogether she found four sewage drainage pipes.

Sandy was afraid the dog had drowned, so down she went, crawling through this ditch. Remember that it was just water, not a sewer. No dog. She went home, but as soon as the sun came up she went out again. She started following some side tributaries and followed them up towards the house, where they disappeared. They had been covered up for over 100 years, but she found them all. Sandy also looked for a golf course, found none, then thought, "Wait a minute. The main ditch goes out to the Pastiche River. Now where this ends and all these little drainage ditches come down to it, across the river is a defunct golf course. They built a golf course and it went under water. There is a fairway right across the river." Sandy ran home to call me and tell me what she had found. I told Sandy, "The dog isn't far away. You are confusing him. Remember dogs don't think in English. They understand intonations. They can picture. If you believe in all the electrical impulses that bring birds home and dogs back, what you are doing is confusing to the dog. You're hysterical. There is this little thing out there, frightened, and if you are mentally sending anything, you are sending terribly frightening things. Clear your mind, concentrate on bringing him home. The things I keep seeing are the barn, willow trees and garage. Bring the dog back."

Sandy sat for hours, and when she went out she would also visualize the little dog and bring him to these trails. Once he found the main trail which led to her house, he couldn't get lost. Now it's Wednesday. Sandy called me. I told her, "I don't see death. He's very quiet, he's very near."

Now it's nearly a week later and it's hunting season. Sandy asked any hunters she saw to please watch out for the dog and to try to bring him home. She called me again and I asked her to come to my house and bring me something the dog had slept on. Joe drove her to my house. By this time she was nearly suicidal. She had no hope, she couldn't tell Donald. She was really at the end. She brought some little dog toys. I looked at her and said, "You have to go on with your life. " I looked at Joe and said to him, "If you don't get her some help I will. She's in very bad shape." This was a nightmare for Sandy. I told Sandy the dog would show up on Sunday. I told her to stop looking for him, he would just show up.

Joe promised he would get her to a psychiatrist and they left. When they arrived home, Sandy called the dog breeder whom they had bought the puppy from and told her the entire story. The breeder said she had another dog. "We won't tell Donald," Sandy and the breeder agreed. The dogs were identical. Maybe they would wait six months and then tell him, or maybe never tell him. She questioned how the breeder could sell her another dog when she had just lost one. The breeder said it was an accident and she knew she didn't do it on purpose. She said, "I'd like to tell you a story about accidents. You've known me about 18 years, but 23 years ago I had a little boy. My husband and I were going to a dinner and I let my sister and brother-in-law take my little boy for the night. He was two years old. In the morning my brother-in-law went for a walk with his German Shepherd and my son. They lived near a park with a lake. They were walking in the park on a cold winter morning. He heard a sound and turned around and the child was gone. He had fallen into the lake, under the ice. He died. Don't tell me about accidents. It wasn't anyone's fault, yet they are still blaming themselves for it." Then the breeder let Sandy have the dog. Now it was Sunday, Joe was afraid to leave her alone, she was so distraught.

At 8:30AM Joe asked her if she would mind staying alone for a few minutes so he could go out to get a newspaper. She said she was not fine, but pulling herself together a bit more, so she thought it would be OK. He came back about 15 minutes later. He's a very laid back person, he doesn't get excited, quiet, gentle and easygoing. Then he walks into the house, voice raised and says to Sandy, "What the hell did you do?" Sandy did not understand and asked what the matter was. He replied, "I don't understand you. I don't believe you're this stupid. You lose a dog, we have spent the last seven days in total torture. Now, we get the other dog, we won't talk about what you had to pay for him, so why would you let the new dog outside alone?" Sandy said, "I didn't let him out." Joe kept yelling, "Why did you let the new puppy out?" Sandy asked, "Out where? Where is he?" Joe answered, "Out in the garage. I drove into the garage and almost hit him. He was sitting there." Sandy was confused but knew there was no way the puppy could have gotten out. They went to the garage and the puppy was still sitting there. Sandy said, "Where is his ear tape? I just did his ears. My God, he's thin." She stared at him and said, "Wait a minute. I think the new puppy is still in the house, asleep. Let me check." Sandy ran into the house and yelled, "Puppy's in here." Joe then asked, "Well then what is this sitting in here? What do you mean he's in there? He's in here. I'm looking right at him." Sandy ran back into the garage with the second puppy and said, "Here he is." Joe asked, "Then what's this? This is weird, it's exactly seven days to the hour that the first puppy was lost. Now we have two puppies, one very thin!"

Sandy ran into the house to call me. Then she called Donald. Two weeks later she drove both puppies to Donald's house in Maryland so he could choose one. They were identical except the lost puppy had a totally different personality from the week before he was lost. He had become assertive, even with the other puppy. The other puppy had been the dominant one in the pack. Donald took the first puppy for a year and showed him. The dog was doing really well. Donald died and his widow was left with the dog. Sandy spoke to her every day and she told her one day that something was wrong with the dog and she didn't know what it was. The dog was getting stranger every day. This was an 80lb. full grown Doberman. Sandy went to Maryland to pick up the dog because he was having separation anxiety. He would rip up the room every time Donald's widow left.

Sandy and Joe now have this dog and his brother, but she has to keep them separated. He is definitely strange. When he is upset he whirls and whirls. Astin, the infamous surrogate mother died. Now if the dog needs to go out and it's raining, he howls and cries and shivers.

A year or so later I was the featured speaker at a kennel club. I spoke to a room full of people about my animal stories. I recognized Sandy and Joe in the audience. After my lecture Sandy stood up and asked if I ever get to meet the people or animals that I have found. I answered, "Very rarely." Sandy said, "Well, I have a treat for you."

Joe brought the Doberman out, a big, friendly dog. He turned him loose. He walked right to me, though we had never met, and stopped dead in his tracks. He looked at me, I patted him and didn't say anything. He walked away to visit some other people. I sat on the floor and then the dog just stopped as if something had happened. He whirled around, all four feet at once, then ran back over to me, climbed into my lap and put his head on my shoulder. Now, in dog language this is totally submissive behavior. It was a body language he had never done with anyone before, Sandy told me. I don't know exactly how the dog knew me, but he knew me. It was like a complete submission to a mother. Sandy has told me in later conversations he has never done this with anyone else since.

CHAPTER ELEVEN
SHEBA'S LOST

Iris Nevins' story:

As Nancy and I were trying to finalize this book, another missing dog story occurred. I have a pack of five Shelties, who live a life of canine luxury on our New Jersey farm. They have three different fenced in yards, totalling about five acres, where they can run and have adventures to their hearts' content. They also have a small old barn for shelter, which is divided into two rooms, and it may well be the largest "dog house" in the whole state. When the sun goes down the dogs come into the main house and spend the evening with the family, sharing tidbits of our dinner (they are terribly spoiled!) and they fall asleep wherever they like. The three males are very protective and sleep in the bedroom at night to keep watch over us.

My friend, Leslie, was dogsitting for her friend Janet's Sheltie, "Sheba". I remember it was a Tuesday, August 23, 1994, when I got a call from Leslie. She had to go out of town and needed someone to watch Sheba and her own dog, Tanner. I am a dog person and consider Tanner one of my best friends. I even taught him how to talk. Whenever I would visit, Tanner would hear my car, come running up to me howling, "I wuw woo, I wuw woo!" Then I would calm him down, and tell him that I loved him, to which he would reply, "I wuw woo woo." I knew he loved me too. I wished I could take him, but unfortunately my three males did not like other males visiting, but I did say I would take Sheba, an adorable little female. I thought she would have a lot of fun with my new little puppy, Juniper.

I had met Sheba a few times before, but she was a nervous dog, and when Leslie brought her over she was a bit frightened by my howling pack of dogs. They were all very curious and it was apparent that Sheba was not enjoying having five other Shelties sniffing at her. Leslie drove off and I took Sheba inside the house to give her some leftover meat. She decided I was OK and followed me outside. I put Sheba and my two females in a separate yard and they seemed to get along peacefully.

I watched the three female dogs for the next hour, bringing more meat out to them several times, making sure Sheba was OK. I felt sure everything was fine, but I had to go out for the afternoon. I knew the dogs couldn't get out of the fence. I drove my car down the driveway and Sheba ran after me along the fence. I got out at the end of the drive and reassured her I would be back in a few hours. She seemed upset that I was leaving, but I thought she would calm down after I left.

When I came back later that afternoon Sheba was gone. We searched all over the huge yard, behind trees and bushes and only found one little spot under the fence where she could have possibly tunnelled under. She may also have climbed the fence. We will never know for sure how she got out.

I called every police station, veterinarian, shelter and animal control person in our own county and every one surrounding. Sheba's owner was off hiking in the woods in Maine and we could not reach her, so I left a message on her answering machine in Pennsylvania, hoping she might call home for her messages. I even called three radio stations in the area and had them make announcements several times a day.

I called Nancy and she said she thought Sheba dug her way out of the fence and was heading home. The poor dog must have been so frightened and confused. I was exhausted from driving all around looking for the dog. Nancy said, "I see that someone will pick her up in two days and bring her back to your house. Right now I see her at an abandoned railroad bed." I thanked her, but could not sit around and wait for someone to return Sheba, so I went to the only abandoned railroad bed I knew of in the area and started to holler "Sheba."

Now it was Tuesday night. We took Buster, our smartest male, out looking for Sheba. If she was around Buster would find her. It was getting dark. There was no sign of Sheba anywhere. I stopped people on bicycles and asked them, but no one had seen her. She was a shy dog and I was afraid she would stay well hidden from anyone who was not familiar.

The next two days were spent looking. It was not until late Wednesday night that I heard from Janet, Sheba's owner. She was very understanding and told me not to blame myself. She said she would drive from Maine the next morning and help look for Sheba. I called Nancy a few more times, and she said Sheba was pretty close by. I thought if she was hiding somewhere on the farm, which has quite a lot of acreage, she might come out if she heard her master's voice.

When Janet arrived Thursday afternoon at about three o'clock, I was a mess. I had hardly eaten or slept since Tuesday. It's bad enough when you lose your own dog, but it's so much worse when it belongs to someone else. Janet called all through the fields and woods, still no Sheba. We decided to get in the car and drive to Leslie's house to see if she made her way back there. As we drove, I told Janet about Nancy and how good she was at finding missing animals. She hoped Nancy was right this time. Nancy had told me to mentally tell Sheba to go to a place where people would see her so she could be picked up and brought back.

A few hours later we were still driving around. We decided we would go to see Nancy with one of Sheba's toys that evening if we didn't find her. We were somehow fairly confident that we would find Sheba. I have kept a phone in my car for the past year or so for emergency use. I use it so infrequently that I was startled when I heard something ringing softly. Janet and I both said, "What's that?" I realized it was the phone. I felt so silly, I didn't even know which button answered the phone for a few seconds. When I answered my daughter was saying, "A trooper just brought Sheba home!" I asked her if she was sure it was Sheba and not another sheltie, and she said she was sure. We called Nancy and told her, and headed back to the farm.

When we got there, Sheba was there, a complete mess, full of burrs. As it turned out a trooper from our local police barracks , the first person I spoke to, was the one to find her. She was picked up about three miles from my house in a small town. The trooper saw a dog that looked like a fox and remembered my description. She wouldn't come to him when he called her name, so he parked his car, opened the back door and sat down in the driver's seat. A minute later, Sheba, who is very used to riding in cars, jumped right in.

Nancy was right again. Just two days later and someone did pick the dog up and bring her back, just as she had seen.

*DIXIE & BABY JUNIPER IN THE
YARD WHERE SHEBA DISAPPEARED*

Reprinted with permission from the Observer Tribune

OBSERVER - TRIBUNE
SEPTEMBER 19, 1985

CHAPTER TWELVE
RACHEL

Gary Micco was on rotation as a detective in 1985 when I first made contact with him.

"I'll start with our initial contact through Ross English." Gary spoke as if no time had passed. "I remember getting a piece of paper with Nancy's name and number on it, everything at the time was so hectic. I had no idea what it was about. We had had this guy, suspect for about 14 hours, and we held him. We had a girl missing but didn't know what happened. We had a dozen people say they saw his car. One lady said she saw him walking in the area where this girl lived. The girl had to walk home that day because she had missed the bus. So we had this guy, we had this girl missing, we didn't know what happened."

The whole thing, how a cop comes in, grabs his daily news and coffee. It starts at 8:00 AM, in sleepy Long Valley. The detective comes to work and starts reading how the Yankees are doing in September and is handed a note to give the Vice-Principal a call on this missing girl that you haven't even gotten as far as reviewing yet. It appeared the day before in the blotter's reports. So you call the Vice-Principal and he says, "What are you doing?" So you say, "What are you talking about? I Didn't get that far yet, it's only 8:05." He said, "She's missing, all of her friends are here, something's wrong." I said, "I'll jump right on it." Then minutes later, I recalled a missing persons report, her parents called, a patrolman followed it up and took the initial report the day before. Might have been a Wednesday. We used to stop traffic and help her cross the street when she was in 8th grade the year before and years prior when she was in the Long Valley Middle School. She passed me on the street coming up here. She used to walk back and forth to that school every day. We have a school post in the morning and afternoon to cross the kids safely. She's the sweetest girl you'll ever meet. Beautiful, she was going to be a Cheryl Tiegs at nineteen. I said, "Runaway? She's so quiet, I didn't know all about her, but she wasn't the kind to run away." Then another note was handed to me by a dispatcher to call a woman from Fairview Avenue which is where Rachel resided. I was supposed to call her. She had information. That was the first indication I had that a young man named Michael Manfredonia was seen in a Green Volvo wagon parked on Fairview Avenue less than a half a mile from Rachel Domas' residence. She described this guy who she thought worked at the local gas station, which at one point he did. Rachel would walk from her home and cut through the gas station towards school. So that was the first contact. Whether it was fascination or what I never asked him.

I went to the man who owns the garage and gas station where Manfredonia worked. He said, "I saw him that day. Matter of fact we were test driving cars on Fairview Avenue, fixing a string of Volvos and I saw his car." Even the guy who worked there said he saw his car parked. Everyone we talked to saw his car. Usually it's the other way around. Usually they say "We've seen nothing." One person saw him walk, so I called the sergeant at Chester Township, and he said, "yeah, we arrested him, (Michael Manfredonia) for receiving stolen property, stolen from the garage where he worked." This may have been why he was terminated. He wasn't an employee there when this happened. (Rachel's disappearance).

So the sergeant said he would dig the file out on Michael. I told him I would stop by on my way to Michael's home. Then he (Michael) called me back and I told him he was seen in the area of this missing girl's residence. He was seen there, his car was seen, we just wanted to know why he was there, trying to take the basic witness approach. Maybe he saw something, the guy was there in the neighborhood for hours. It had to be minutes later I got another call from the sergeant, he said, "He's here." I said, "What?" He said, "He's here at headquarters and he's saying he wants to know what the status of his community service is that he's been working off for a radar detector arrest. And I'm thinking, I said, "Hang on to him, I want to talk to him." So I went down, introduced myself, "Would you help me out here, explain to me, would you come to my headquarters with me, and explain to me what you were doing the whole time." He wrote this statement, two pages long, hand-written on how he was traveling down Fairview Avenue, left his house in Chester to go to the Quik-Chek in Flanders, off

Bartley Road, to get cigarettes and soda. Drove back, took Bartley, then went to Nauright and down Fairview. His car broke down, he walked around for help. He went to the gas station for help. Then he left. I'm reading this and I say, "Hey wait, how does your car break down? It was parked up a hill, off the road, a little wood road that went nowhere, about 200 feet long. How does your car break down, you back up a hill after it breaks down, you walk aimlessly a couple of hours, you start up your car after that and you drive home. What happened, and I'll never forget reading that statement which he signed, made the hair stand up on the back of my neck. There is something so wrong. No one was thinking murder. No one. This is the morning, 11:00 AM, it began at 8:00 AM, so we had our guy at around 11:AM. I called George Deuchar, he and I were both in the detective bureau, and I said to him, "Get here now." He said he was right in the middle of Fire Prevention at a school. "Get here now, we have a problem. Drop what you're doing." He showed up. We held him, (Michael), gave him a phone book, said, "If you want a lawyer, go look." I opened it up to L and ceased questioning. We fed him, took care of him, held him, just detained him. We couldn't help but connect him to Rachel, his vehicle had been there, everyone said she missed the bus, a couple of neighbors said they saw her walking, one person saw her walking towards her house and saw Michael walking towards her. You've got him telling a bizarre story of how his car broke down. The prosecutor's office got involved. They looked for Rachel by checking the area by helicopter, cars and on foot. Hours went by, we got nowhere. We drove him home, we had to let him go. That's a vast area we checked, woods, fields, cornfields, rivers. Long walk, she walked a couple of miles from the High School. So at what point did she disappear? I felt, using common sense, that I knew where they would have met if they both walked at a normal pace. But it was not true. He never got a lawyer. What happened was that we had exhausted him. We held him for fourteen hours and George Deuchar and I brought him home. We held his car, took it and processed it. We didn't have a crime. I believe part of the case was lost, because it had two phases. The first was a missing person's case then a kidnapping. We let him go about 5:00 AM and George and I drove back to that area, the railroad bend, everything, you could just feel it in your bones. I think it was probably that day, that holding time when I was handed a note to call Nancy.

When I called her she said she had seen a photo of Rachel, given to her by a neighbor and she had to see me. Nancy told me she knew Rachel was dead, murdered.

We didn't even know. We had no body. Nancy said his name, talked about his wandering eye and said he worked at a gas station. Nancy said she could see him taking her and dragging her.

Nancy continues.......

Having Gary speak about those days brought events rolling back. While Gary was busy putting the pieces together, I was receiving a phone call that moved my day into high gear.

"Mary, hi, yes, I think I know who you are. You came to a workshop I gave in Long Valley. What can I do for you?"

She quickly went on, "A neighbor and friend's daughter is missing, her name is Rachel Domas. Do you get anything?"

When I didn't respond she continued: "Would a photo help?"

Sunken, I couldn't figure out a way to say no. I felt I already knew what happened to Rachel. I didn't necessarily know what to do with the horror I was seeing.

"Sure, I like to verify what I see in my mind. A photo will help Can you come over sometime today?"

Click, conversation over, my day totally altered. Mary was on her way over with a school year book. I had about a half hour before human tragedy would once more sit in my psyche reminding me that I was part of a species that I was mostly saddened by. Less than an hour later she was at my door. After seeing the photo in the year book I ran to call Ross English. I told him I knew of a missing girl and named her. He asked if I knew what happened to her. I said, "Yes." He asked if I could tell him the circumstances surrounding her disappearance. Again, "Yes." "Is someone there making it difficult to talk." "Absolutely," I answered, glad that he understood. "Get her out of the room and I'll call you back in a few minutes," we hung up.

Mary was moved into the living room while I went back to my office to supposedly meditate.

When I called Ross back his opening line was, "I just got off the phone with the detectives on the case and they don't have a clue. What do you have?"

Going back to my first images when Mary called this morning, I related exactly what I received.

"She's been murdered. He, the kid who killed her, worked around the corner from her but they hardly ever spoke. He's the kid no parents let their children be with. He's different, not part of any crowd, always alone. Left school last year, worked at a local garage pumping gas. Special educational needs but mostly emotional. He saw her walking past the wooded lot going home from school and hated her. She represented everybody who ever made fun of him or snubbed him. He grabbed her and she resisted. He's much stronger than her, he took her by the throat and dragged her into the mountainous woods where he promptly killed her. Her body is still there, I can show you where. Sorry, almost forgot, his name is Michael and there is something wrong with one eye. Father drives a pickup truck. That's all I got."

"They just found her body...in the woods...no evidence around and...they picked up Michael for questioning this morning but without a body they had to let him go. Now they can't find him." Ross finished his side of the information.

"I can find him easily. Poor kid, what a mess." Two families now devastated. Lots of dear friends would mourn a sweet young girl's horrible meeting with death. So unfair, I never quite make sense out of the pain of it all. All those metaphysicians who talk about everyone choosing their path have never been a crime victim.

No one chooses that path, no one except the perpetrator who couldn't possibly be listening to their own soul.

I remember when I was six years old when we moved to a new neighborhood in the East Flatbush section of Brooklyn. Our two bedroom brick house was one of many squeezed together in a three block development called Dodgertown. I knew it would be ours the moment I saw it. I loved it and remember claiming it by using the bathroom. It wasn't until years later that my parents told me that they went house hunting without any hope of purchasing for years. They wanted to dream. When they found this house they put reason aside, and a $5.00 down payment made it ours. We moved in three months later.

Moving day came, and at 6 years of age I wasn't of much help. A boy and girl rang our bell and asked to play with me. I suppose my parents felt grateful to them and let me go outside. I didn't want to. I hated meeting new people. It was hard to leave my best friends, Linda and Harriet. They were one year younger than me but they played catch and jump rope with me every day until we moved. I loved to play with them, we all cheered each other on. We were a happy family. Linda and Harriet were fraternal twins. Linda was our leader, she had great ideas and we were happy to go along with them. Now I was sitting on the first porch I ever sat on with strangers. I could hardly hear them and I didn't want to talk. I remember them telling me they lived across the street, next door to each other. I was so shy I didn't say a word. They kept talking and I kept hoping it would be over so I could see my new room being set up. My sister Anita and I would share the room, just like before.

I watched them as they turned to watch another boy walk past us on the street. The boy sitting next to me called out, "There goes four eyes," and the girl laughed. My shyness was thrown out by my fury. I knew what it meant.

"If you are going to talk like that you can't stay here with me," I yelled at them. Everyone has a handicap, only some you can see and some you can't. Don't make fun of anyone in front of me. I don't like it."

My voice was the loudest I had ever heard it. I sat, surprised at my voice and the thoughts that darted out of my mouth. They must have wondered what planet I came from but all they did was agree I was right. They muttered an apology to me and I said, "I'm not the one you hurt." I was still furious. It was the first time I ever remembered being angry. They called out, "Sorry," loud enough for the other boy to hear and then quickly left. I had not made any friends that day. I sat on the porch for awhile, wondering how I knew all that. I knew it was different from my regular thoughts. More like the stuff "the man" spoke of. I was very proud of my discovery. It was nice to care. Maybe I wasn't the selfish child my mother told me I was. I jumped off the porch and skipped into the house. I didn't care if anyone liked me, I liked myself. It was a discovery that planted a seed that took decades to grow.

In the fourth grade I suddenly began walking with a limp. My hip hurt almost all the time. My parents took me to our family physician who could not find anything. His conclusion was I was faking it to get attention. He had admitted my sister to a hospital earlier that year. She had polio in the legs. The only explanation he could come to was that I mimicking her. He told my parents I probably needed some attention. Although the limp faded over the next few months and my parents assumed he was right, years later in reviewing a spinal tomogram I could see the congenital deformities that led to my limp. It was only my devotion from age three to the field of classical ballet that kept my muscles sufficiently strong and stretched enough to balance and compensate for the spine and missing disc tissue. Every family has their stories. The story told about my childhood by the adults was that the only thing I ever really asked for were dancing lessons. I started asking at age two and by three they gave in. Perhaps my inner teacher was working through me even then. These lessons that I took until age 13 taught me to instinctually understand movement. This has served to help me learn to restore function again and again despite extensive injuries incurred at the hands of others. I believe my love and devotion to the dance has literally kept me out of a wheelchair.

I've always considered myself fortunate. With all the possibilities that present themselves, I've never lost the ability to care for myself and others. I believe that may be why I can feel Michael and his issues and can feel Rachel and her pain.

Ross's voice continued, "Don't tell the woman. They have to tell the parents first." Ross clicked off.

Mary was in the living room. I joined her and looking straight into her eyes I said:

"Mary, there is nothing we can do at the moment. Please go home, if I can, I will call you later."

I turned my back quickly in case she could see past my frozen eyes, trying to hide what I knew.

Detective Gary Micco called a few minutes later. He and his partner were the guys who let Michael go. He wanted to know: "Do you know where Michael is?"

"I need to meet with you, I have to draw it on a paper. Can't just tell you."

"I have to ask the prosecutor. He'll be here later. I'll call back."

Click. Goodbye. Time to cook dinner now. Staring at the open refrigerator, no inspiration came. Moved to the pantry, no flash of inspiration there either. Stop and just move your head, Nancy. Just a little to the left of murder and perhaps an appetite to feed love will come back. Your children do need to eat, and you know you'll eat anything just to stuff down the horrible images.

The call came several hours later. Shyly Gary said:

"The prosecutor said no go. My boss said to do whatever I needed. Can't you just tell him where Michael is?"

My mule kicked in: "No, I can't explain why, but it has to be in person."

I don't know how much was my hurt ego and how much is this weird ability that comes along with being psychic. I'm "told" what circumstances are necessary for work, sometimes I need the scene, sometimes the quiet of my room and sometimes a long drive away from everything. This time I knew I needed to be face to face with Gary Micco.

Desparate, Gary called back an hour later. "Can you meet me at 10:00 PM? We can meet halfway. You know the church off Nauright?"

A sucker for intrigue, I blurted, "Sure."

A friend was staying with us and agreed to watch the children. I started out in my children's play pen on wheels...the station wagon. It was on its last legs but had never let me down. I always felt safe in it but tonight I was incredibly nervous. I had agreed to meet a stranger late at night in a dark place. By the time I arrived at the parking lot my imagination had destroyed my nervous system. I was terrified. His white car with the red bubbles on top helped calm me. I pulled up alongside, and with handbag in hand, got in the front seat of his car. The interior was lit. He was young and good looking in a soft way. No hardened tough cop look. His eyes seemed to have a depth of concern and intelligence. I was glad to hear a bit of anxiety in his voice:

"Do you mind if I look through your purse?"

Handing him my bag I realized he was as terrified as I was, with a lot more at stake. The relief on his face was as obvious as his smile. No hidden gun or microphone to catch him. We sat and talked trivia for a few minutes, searching for the links that would comfort each of us and help us feel on familiar ground. A John Lennon song came on the radio:

"One of my favorite people," Gary remarked.

My smile showed we found a mutual space to share. Within minutes I took a pen and paper out of my bag and showed him where a piece of her jewelry and torn clothing could be found. He now understood why I couldn't tell him. The evidence was in hundreds of acres of hilly woods. I included several garbage cylinders and an idea of what particular garbage was lying on the ground. He couldn't miss it.

"Where is Michael?"

"Whoops, he's ill. He took an overdose of some over the counter sedative to kill himself. He wants to go home. He's on a hilltop looking down at his home. He's waiting to see his father's truck. He'll come down when his father comes home. He needs him. Wait a minute, his house is being watched. It's a bunch of cop cars. You know his house is being watched, don't you?"

"Yes, but how do you know?"

"I'm seeing it with a different kind of...he's starting to come down the hill...there's his dad's car. He's walking slowly, drugged and sick. He's coming near..."

The car radio blasted a call I couldn't make out. I understood it must have been a call for Gary and all others to come to the capture because he started up his car slow enough for me to jump out. I could hear the wind whistling as he left the lot. I stood in the dark suddenly alone. Murder already committed carries its own current of terror that lasts long after the deed. Years later I still am haunted by the images of what one human being can do in the name of hatred and fear. I jumped into my car and as quickly as possible, drove home.

Not ready to face the dreams that might await me, I went to my office and did some very practical work, paying bills and sorting letters. Kept my head moving in a direction as far away as possible from the terror. When my body ached with the need to lay down, I conceded and went to bed. I hoped to shed the images but all night Rachel's sweet face and being kept calling for comfort. So did Michael's, only his face was a distorted look that went beyond terror. It must have hit him with a force, one explosive rage, over in minutes, enough to do a lifetime of damage to Rachel's family and friends. Enough to irrevocably remove Rachel from life as we know it.

Lucid dreams have been my way for the longest time. While the dream takes place, my conscious self is able to notice that I am dreaming. Sometimes I will be busy interpreting the messages while the dream occurs. Tonight I just prayed to help one very gentle sweet soul who did not have a chance to say good-bye to her loved ones. Her dreams were shattered far more than mine no matter how horrid my dreams.

Glad for morning, I kept waiting for some call, some acknowledgment of the strange moments Gary and I shared, no calls, no feedback. I opened my front door and picked up the local paper. The headlines spoke of Michael's capture and an ambulance ride he took to the nearest hospital where they pumped his stomach. He had attempted suicide with a non-prescription drug.

I did not call Gary nor did he call me. Much later in the year I again read about the Rachel Domas case when Michael was brought to trial. He was found guilty and given a life sentence.

About a year later I was out dancing with friends. My house sat up on a hill. A quick walk down the hill brought us to the Mount Olive Inn, a local bar with bands playing on Thursday, Friday and Saturday evenings,. Every Thursday after teaching meditation class, some of the students would go with me. Tonight was different; it was a Friday and the place was packed. Movement was more a shove, a push, excuse me please.

A glass of cheap white wine in hand, I carefully threaded my way from the bar to the wall eight feet away. A friend, Frank was there. Frank and I met one year at a Christmas party given by the local paper, the Mount Olive Chronicle.

Now years later, he was looking at me through his metal rimmed glasses with a question mark in his eyes.

"Nancy, remember that Long Valley murder last year, the young girl? It had the hand of Nancy written all over it. You worked on it, didn't you?"

"Frank you know I never discuss crime cases."

With a big smile, I kissed him on the cheek and quickly turned towards the dance floor.

"Sorry," I said as I nudged someone's back with my shoulder.

"It's okay," the voice said and turning towards me we both smiled. Gary Micco was enjoying his first night out at the Mt. Olive Inn.

"Nancy, I've been wanting to talk with you, let's go to the back where it's quieter."

Gary led the way. Past the bar were a group of booths. Traditional dark red vinyl cushions on hard wood benches formed some privacy. They were as far as you can get from the music without stepping outside.

"I felt terrible afterwards. The prosecutor absolutely did not want any publicity with a psychic."

"Even if I was right?"

"I never told him. I went with your map the next day and collected the evidence exactly as you said. Even the garbage was what you said it would be. Tom had taken pills to kill himself. Everything was as if you were there. When I put the evidence on the prosecutor's desk he said, "See, you didn't need her.""

(For a recounting of this case and Gary Micco's other work with Nancy, see Appendix F)

CHAPTER THIRTEEN
A VISION OF MURDER

"Enid, I feel awful, I see a husband killing his wife."
Enid and I were mutual friends of Shirley and Harvey. We were paying them a visit.

"My god, not Shirley and Harvey?" Enid's face turned a shade paler than I had ever seen.

"No, not them, it's wierd, it feels like it is connected to them somehow. I can't tell who though."

We had pulled up to their house. I attempted to recover my balance and we went in to spend a peaceful lunch in a beautiful, mountainous area of New Jersey where we could see miles of greenery. That night lying in bed I couldn't stop thinking of the thought of a husband killing a wife. The next day I called Shirley and told her what was obsessing my every moment. She had no information to add except that she was glad it wasn't about them.

That was in the middle of August, 1986. Seven days later I was driving alone to Shirley and Harvey's. All gone I thought. No more murder feelings. Getting out of my car, no need to lock it here, I walked up to the glass door. Harvey was standing there with a strange unreadable face. "Ellen was murdered this morning. Brad and Robin are devastated. Would you go talk with them?" Reeling from the impact, I now knew all the pieces. Ellen, this is told for all the gentle and innocent people of the world.

Back in July of 1986 Shirley and I were lounging by her pool when she suggested we walk over to her neighbor's house to meet a new employee, hired directly from China. "Her name is Ellen, she's 40 years old, sweet and special. We were told that she has wanted to come to America since she was a little girl. Would you like to meet her.?" Ellen was outside talking with Brad and Robin when we were introduced. I walked over to her smiling and she ran into my arms. I held her to me and when we broke apart we walked arm in arm into the house. We did not speak the same verbal language, but obviously we communicated deeply with each other. I left her my number on a slip of paper and told her if she ever wanted company please call. We were friends. Walking out I remember Shirley's strange look and comment, "I've never seen someone of Chinese descent so effusive with someone they just met." That was the only time Ellen and I were to be together.

As I drove to the next driveway and pulled up all I could think of was I didn't realize she had been married. She had to be, in my mind it was a wife murder. Brad and Robin told me what they could. Ellen was driven in to Brooklyn, NY that morning. Her husband (a marriage arranged via letter to allow entry into America) had agreed to annul the as yet unconsummated marriage. She had also agreed to pay him a sum of $500 a month for several months. When Charlie, a friend of Brad's drove her in, Mr. Wang, her husband, asked Charlie to please wait downstairs. I don't know why he agreed to; Ellen was afraid of Mr. Wang, as I later had confirmed for me. But history is history. Charlie went downstairs, and with much forethought, Mr. Wang took a knife and butchered a lovely and gentle woman. He then called the police and told them they had an argument that led to a violent quarrel. As I listened all I could do was console them and remind them that whatever time Ellen had in America, her dream had come true. We agreed that I would come back in a few days and look at the situation. This was being done in friendship, there was an understanding that there was to be no monetary consideration for any work I would do for them.

Three days later my daughter accompanied me to their home. It was warm with a soft breeze so we all decided the back deck was where we all wanted to be. I started, "Mr. Wang had hurt her before, didn't he? In fact, I feel he had been here."

"Yes, we found him lurking around and then found out that he went into Ellen's quarters and made her sleep in a chair while he slept in the bed. He then tried to strangle her. She came crying to us and we threw him off the property."

"Good, then there is a police report." That would make my work go easier."

"No, we didn't call the police. He left."

"But he tried to kill her then. Okay, listen, it's still important that the Brooklyn D. A. 's office is told this information."

"Why should I tell them that?"

"Because it's proof that it was premeditated and that it was
not a case of domestic dispute. He will try to prove it as domestic,
you have to fight him on it. Otherwise, bail could be affordable and
he'd be out."

"Do you think that he would come back here? Don't say he
would." Robin's scared voice cut in.

"Robin, do you want me to tell you what I believe and feel,
or do you want me to shut up? I know it's frightening, but it's more
frightening when you don't deal with what you have. Then you
have no control at all. Mr. Wang would love to steal from you, he
saw your place. Your best protection is a high bail. He'll never get
out or even get to trial. I see him dying of a heart attack in jail. If
you don't help, he could get out and then I would suggest you have
your place under round-the-clock guard."

"Stop talking like that. Why do you want me frightened?"
Robin was pregnant and even more sensitive than usual.

"Robin, I didn't kill Ellen, I'm trying to help resolve it. Do
whatever you want, but I wouldn't pretend this man would only
harm Ellen and no one else."

With that Rebecca and I left. "Are they stupid or what?"
Rebecca's voice echoed my disbelief in how wrapped up in self pres-
ervation they were. Amazing how blind to the effects they were. If
only they had called the police the first time. Even if nothing else
would have been accomplished, they would have clearly come to
terms with not letting her go upstairs alone to that man's apartment. How could they? My voice got loud and furious. Ellen died

because no one had the courage to take action against a nasty, vicious individual.

A week later Brad sent me a copy of his letter to the DA's office. He believed me. He did find out that Mr. Wang had told his barber days before that he was going to kill his wife.

Bail was set high and Mr. Wang could not post it. Several weeks later Brad called to tell me that Mr. Wang died in jail of a heart attack.

The next message I received was that Robin gave birth to their first child. Happy for them and glad that the worst was behind them I drove to their place once again, this time a gift for a new life in hand.

Robin sat up in bed and sternly told me, "It's your fault I had a C-section. You're guilty of ruining my time."

"Robin, you have a problem, but I'd look a little closer if I were you. You're terrified and could use some help. I didn't do it to you. "

Knowing she could say it because she only cared about a very small world that began and ended with her, I promptly left never to return. I paid a very small price for their fear, we'll never know if Ellen's' murder could have been stopped if they had acted on the first attempt. The only consolation I live with is my belief that everything happens in a complex, grand design larger than I can imagine.

Ellen's situation and death brought childhood pains to the surface. I always felt like a stranger where everyone else knew life. What I experienced filled me with shyness, thinking that I was peculiar.

I grew up hearing a deep and loving male voice that no one else could hear. The voice would tell me all sorts of things...when people would be born, when people would die; world and local events weeks and years before they would happen. That voice was to come back to me at 31 years of age.

When he would speak, it was so different from the fear of my mother, sometimes insinuating, sometimes telling me I was crazy.

I had no idea what I was crazy about. All the things told to me by "the man" came true. I kept him a secret. He was so much a part of my life that I never doubted he existed. No one else ever saw him, I never knew his name then, and I never thought to question him. He spoke in a loving, non-judgmental way. I had never heard anyone speak like he did. He just said things. No sarcasm, no mean or scared looks, and no yelling. Just the truth. It felt so good to hear things told to me that didn't leave me feeling stupid and scared.

Years later I could look back and see what a powerful model that was. I didn't have the words for what happened. I only knew it left me comforted to be spoken with as an equal about important things that mattered to myself and others. I had a secret life and it felt special. It was a world only I could visit and I could feel good there. My teacher liked me no matter who was angry at me or punishing me. He was always telling me that he cared by sharing grown up stuff with me. I was very impressed but didn't dare ask anybody who he might be. They might try to steal him or take me away from him. Not that they could, they couldn't see him. But somehow they would try to destroy my special time. Just like they did with ballet.

My mother used to tell a story that goes something like this: "The only thing Nancy ever asked for was ballet lessons. By the time she was three we gave in. She never asked for anything else, just ballet."

The first dancing school was okay, nothing exciting. My little body was getting bored. Where is the real stuff? Then my teacher suggested that I be enrolled in Mrs. Anderson's class in the St. Felix Street Playhouse. It was right down the road from the Brooklyn Academy of Music. Just putting on my shoes and waiting for the signal to begin class was enough to speed my heart into racing gear. The smell of toe shoes was just around the corner. Soon I could dance on stage with all the other dedicated dancers. Any movie that had song and dance I would watch with rapture, carefully study the moves. After classes on Saturdays I could hardly move. It was a happy exhaustion, and I would repeat the situation every day and anywhere I could for years. The basement of our home was my retreat, on went the record player, on went the ballet shoes, and into my heart went Anna Pavlova. Then one day I saw the movie

Singing In The Rain. Heaven opened up its pearly gates. I jumped onto chairs, leaped onto the couch and flew into a frenzy of classical ballet, modern dance and rock and roll. Could anything be better?

One day, the magic I yearned for arrived. Years of waiting and now the pink shoes. Tying pink ribbons around my ankles was like the God and the Goddess embracing at my feet. My feet were no longer of flesh and blood. I loved the callous on each big toe. Treasures that reassured me I was on my way to becoming Anna Pavlova's spiritual sister. I walked through our house on point, then on ice skates, then on point. Couldn't I wear these to school? I spent hours spinning on point, could I really fly into another world? It produced the purest joy I had ever known. And it did for as long as it lasted.

At thirteen I was told I was ready to try out for Carnegie Hall classes in preparation for the American Ballet Corp. My dream was coming true. Nothing else mattered, I could get through everything if I could just dance my life.

Tryouts were terrifying. I was the youngest person in the room, all the others looked at least seventeen. There were only about eight people, including young men. My heart leaped higher than my legs as I flew across the room with as much grace as I could summon.

I made it, I now attended Carnegie Hall classes. The first few lessons were hard. I loved it, it showed me how much more I could learn. Every move, every breath while in those magical slippers fed my soul.

Going home one day my mother brought up the subject of money.

"We just can't afford the lessons. I guess if we really had to, we could take out a loan, but that would be costly to us and I don't know if we could pay it back."

"Of course, mom, if you can't, you can't. I understand."

I have no idea what I understood. Maybe the ice that formed around my mind kept me from feeling the loss. The dreams left that day not to return for years. A large mental iceberg formed sometime during the years I spent in nursing school. My mother one day casually remarked to a friend:

"Oh, we had the money for ballet, but we did not want our daughter to be a dancer."

When I read the *Emperor's New Clothes* it melted a piece of the ice to know that someone else felt the way I did. I finally found someone just like me. The author of that tale saw just the way I saw and no one liked him for it either. That meant he could understand what I was going through. I had another friend. I never met this friend, but after that I felt a little safer and happier just knowing someone somewhere understood. I never shared my secret as a child but I knew there must be others like me, if only I could figure out how to find them. I wouldn't understand or find them until I was 31. It took decades to shed most of the shyness that had captured me early on. Ellen did not have the opportunity to live long enough to shed hers.

❧❧❧

Reprinted with permission of The Daily Record

DAILY RECORD
JANUARY 3, 1988

CHAPTER FOURTEEN
MURDER CLOSE TO HOME

A local detective called to ask me if I would take a look at the recent murder of a 42 year old divorcee. The police had some interesting leads and were curious to see if my psychic vision would match their hunches. This case was close to home. It was a woman I had seen in the local bar where I danced regularly. A group of friends would join me once a week and we would dance until closing. Great exercise and wonderful fun. We wouldn't be looking for men but it was a place, as bars go, where men and women would check each other out.

I didn't know the woman, but remembered her face. Pretty lady. Not so pretty were the photos of her brutal murder. As usual, the police would not tell me anything. As usual, I asked if I could go to the murder scene. It was strange going there. I had lots of friends in that apartment complex. Walking there with the police into a blocked off apartment made me aware of how unsafe the world can be.

As I walked from the car I had a nasty feeling that I could feel as a physical sense. I knew it was not coming from inside me, rather as something off towards my right. I turned towards that direction and saw a gazebo. As I stared a grayish cloud filled shape that I knew to be a male was standing there. It was the energy image of a killer. I could tell by the jaggedness and discoloration of the field. I had my first clue. I tuned into the energy and started directing questions to it, knowing that it was my relay transmission link to the mind of the killer. The first question I asked it was, if he knew the victim. No, only familiar with watching her. The unconscious mind to mind link does not frighten even criminals if it is done lovingly. They will not shield from it as long as it does not pose a threat. I kept my heart open as I worked knowing love is the strongest and best tool I could ever use in working with anyone on anything.

This all took place in the space of time needed to walk about 50 feet to the door of the apartment. Other police from the state were there. They were ready to listen, though not necessarily believe, but I was used to that. I walked around the apartment and although I didn't show emotion, a wave of horror and sadness swept over me as I saw the after effects of the crime.

The woman's body had been removed, but the blood remained all over the living room wall from floor to ceiling. Her teenage daughter heard something in her sleep and went out into the living room only to discover her mother lying against the living room wall with blood everywhere. She ran out of the apartment screaming. Walking into her daughter's room my eyes went to the ceiling. It was covered with angry writing in red expressing hatred and fury at her mother. I smiled and remembered when I let my daughter crayon her bedroom wall in our apartment. Her mother was very understanding also.

I walked back into the living room , ready to share what I felt and saw. "It was a young man who uses drugs, roams at night, was high when he killed her, and never met her although he may have at one point met her daughter briefly and probably saw her out at some bar. He lives in Netcong. He came in through the kitchen window fast. Too fast for her to do anything. He immediately attacked her. He was looking for someone to cut up. He's done quite a few petty crimes, mostly stealing."

The police obviously felt differently. They were talking now. They were torn between it being the daughter, whom they felt hated her mother, and thought her mother was a tramp. Or one of the mother's string of lovers. Not so, I told them. She did not sleep around. She was searching for a permanent relationship and did not always choose wisely. Who does? She was honest enough to admit it and break it off when she realized it was not right for her.

I continued: "She tried to maintain friendships with the men after she left and some of them were still her friends. It did not mean she slept with them any longer. Her daughter was going through difficulties over not having a family life and normal mother daughter issues." The police and I obviously clashed on our opinions. They reiterated that she played around and probably let in "one of her many lovers. She was a tramp." I had not heard that word since adolescence. They would not be easy to convince. I let it go and told them to take me home. It would be pointless to fight their beliefs about women.

Not being believed came naturally to me. Years of therapy and meditation had erased most of the pain, but nothing would ever remove the memories. As we walked out a part of me was back in the fifth grade standing outside P.S. 168 in Brooklyn, refusing to walk home from school. My friends tried to get me to go home but all I would tell them was, "I'm waiting for the limo to take me to the United Nations. I have work to do there." I kept seeing this man step out of a limo and hold the door open for me as I walked out of the U.N. I recognized the line of flags and the building from photographs in a school book. Someone snitched and told my teacher. She called my mother. By then my family definitely thought I was odd. Not a word about it did I hear. Years later I heard that I was considered a pathological liar for telling that story.

In 1986, some 30 years later I worked on a project at the United Nations. I brought in some friends to help, one of them suggested calling someone they knew to expand on our project. Next thing I knew a man named Brian called to volunteer his time. We agreed to meet at a hotel 25 minutes east of where I lived. I pulled up to the hotel parking lot, parked my car and got out. Brian was waiting at the entrance. We shook hands and he took the car keys out of his pocket. He offered to drive. We walked until he stopped at the door of a stretch limo. Brian and his father are owners of a fleet of limos. He noticed how I kept staring at him, his face was familiar but I couldn't place it. We went to the UN and he left a few minutes before me. I was still saying my good-bye. I walked out as I approached him; I saw the street of flags waving, the limo and Brian opening the door, waiting for me. It all came rolling back. I was outside PS 168 seeing exactly the same thing.

In the sixth grade, my teacher sexually molested me when he asked me to stay after class and help. I was the teacher's pet...how fortunate. My teacher grabbed me and held me tight with one hand while the other went up my skirt and into my panties. I shouted and tried to pull away. He held me from behind, tighter and tighter. Someone banged on the door hearing the noise. My teacher jumped away, the door opened as the janitor inquired if everything was all right, I ran past him and all the way home. It took about 32 years to wipe the fear out when I'm approached by a male from behind. I had been through therapy and hypnosis, but nothing stopped the terror except my husband Dick's love that wrapped itself around me the first time he approached me from behind to hold me. It melted the fear like a fire to ice.

I did what 99% of all abused children do...nothing. At least nothing anyone noticed. In the fifth grade I had made friends and had found my voice, now I retreated completely. I could not figure out what I had done to be so punished. The world was not safe anywhere I went. Two weeks later I was informed that I was not going to enter a special program the next year, the S. P. class (they skip a year). My best friend along with the rest of my classmates would go into the program. Three of us did not make it. I went from feeling bad to knowing I was also very stupid. A caterpillar couldn't weave a tighter cocoon. Nancy Zangwill, the only friend I was still talking with walked home with me. She started crying. Her tears broke my wall and I poured out what had happened, concluding with "he hates me, I thought he liked me." We were crying when my sister came in. I couldn't speak. My girlfriend told Anita what happened, all of it.

That night I heard my sister, mother and father talking loudly in the basement. Anita told them everything. They said they would speak to the principal. No one spoke with me. I went to sleep. Now I call them power dreams, then I called them nightmares. I would wake up screaming in a cold sweat, unable to move. Seeing the frightening images of snakes surrounding my bed, crawling out of every pipe in the house, just waiting for me, reaching out for me. It would take hours to stop shaking. The next day I waited for one of my parents or my sister to talk with me. Days went by, I had to go into that class again and again and see his face. I was afraid to breathe and miss the change that was bound to come. It still hadn't. I went into the seventh grade a frozen, frightened child, feeling stupid and left out. Before that year I never thought about grades. I loved to study and learn. During seventh grade I barely passed my subjects, never participated, wouldn't talk to anyone and did not believe I would ever feel differently. In the 8th grade a wonderful man named Mr. David Jacobson changed all that. In less than five minutes his love and kindness undid a world of harm. Mr. Jacobson was my history and english teacher. About the second month of school, he asked to speak to me after class. I came up to his desk and he gently questioned me.

"Nancy, is there something upsetting you? You are so bright and your answers in class and on paper are some of the best I've ever seen. But you always appear to be sad. You can tell me."

Me, smart? Couldn't be. Mr. Jacobson also had the reputation of being the hardest marker in the school. He never gave above a 90, everyone said.

"I'm not in the special advance class. All my friends are." I barely looked at him as I spoke.

"But Nancy, you are as bright as them. I wondered why you weren't allowed to go."

As he spoke he pulled out a manilla folder with my name on the side. I will never forget his showing it to me. He knew I needed proof.

"It shows here your sixth grade teacher refused to sign for you as a candidate for entrance. Why? What happened between the two of you?"

And so, he was the first adult I ever told. When we finished his tears and gentleness helped heal a large hole in my heart and my psyche. That year I was the proud recipient of the only 95 ever given by Mr. Jacobson. I met his wife, visited their home and visited him every year thereafter until a spinal injury and surgery at age 21 prohibited travelling. By the time I could go, he had retired. If anyone knows what happened to Mr. David Jacobson of P.S. 232, Winthrop Jr. High, Brooklyn, NY, please drop me a line, I'd love to know. I always send him my love. Today I share as much back as I can by developing manuals, tapes and workshops on self-esteem for teachers and students. It's my thank you to a kind and loving teacher.

Back to the murder at hand. The detective and I got into his olive green chevy. He looked at me and said, "You don't think it was the daughter?"

"Not at all," was my reply.

Not only was the daughter devastated by the mother's murder, with plenty of her own guilty feelings (I believed they had just argued that day), but she was a definite suspect in their eyes! I spoke to the detective about my concern and the girl's need for help. Not knowing who killed her mother, she had to be pretty terrified for her own life. That was the first and last meeting on the case for me.

Through friends who were working as local reporters I heard that the daughter was given a lie detector test and passed. No other word came until approximately 3 months later when a 19 year old Netcong resident was picked up for petty theft and later confessed to the murder. He was booked and found guilty of first degree murder. The report told of his drug history.

Months later at a lecture I was giving, I spoke about the lack of intuition and compassion on the part of those particular officers. A woman came up to me when the lecture was finished. She was a close friend of the dead woman's family and thanked me. The daughter was so traumatized by not only the murder, but by authorities who believed she was possibly guilty, that she left the state. I was also told that she became a recluse, unable to communicate with the outside world. Wherever she is I pray for her healing to take place. She has suffered far more than anyone deserves.

One day perhaps law enforcement agents will be taught the spiritual aspects of serving a community and the benefits of using one's intuition coupled with an objective, non-judgmental attitude.

Reprinted with permission from the Daily Record

MORRIS COUNTY DAILY RECORD
NOVEMBER 28, 1982

FBI lab used to track murder suspect

Murder suspect possesses long history of arrests

This is the Brentwood Gardens apartment complex in Wharton, where murder suspect James Koedatich worked as a superintendent for about two weeks. The superintendent's office is on the first floor in the center of the photo.

Reporter recalls suspect's gunfight

Reprinted with permission from the Daily Record

DAILY RECORD CONTINUED

CHAPTER FIFTEEN
SERIAL KILLER

"Hi, Nancy, this is Louise. You may not remember me. We met at Margaret's house this summer," the voice on the phone said.

I'm always grateful when someone gives me a clue so I can put a face to the voice.

"My daughter Katy's best friend, Amy Hoffman, is missing. Amy worked last night at the Morris County Mall, and her car was found there with the door open."

In the summer of 1982, my friend Margaret, whom I have known since the eighth grade, invited me to her daughter's Bat Mitzvah. Leaving the temple, we followed them back to their house where I promptly piled food on a paper plate. With drink in one hand and chipmunk cheeks, I grinned my hello to a couple who introduced themselves as Dr. George and Louise Williams (not their real names).

George has a PhD. in psychology, and Louise was attending Rutgers University in New Jersey. She was studying a rare tumor as part of her thesis in microbiology. Louise was excited to talk to a psychic and George was squinting his disbelief. She had heard me on a radio show with Candy Jones about a month earlier. I was impressed with her memory.

Months went by, and the summer heat had changed to a brisk cold chill. I was preparing Thanksgiving dinner for my children and myself when the phone rang.

As she spoke an image drifted dead center where I could not hide from it. A naked body was lying in a tank of water, bruises pointed to a painful end. Her dark hair hid her face, but I knew her name.

"Louise, if I can be of any help, the best thing to do is if you will call the police in your town and tell them I will be more than willing to work with them directly. I will give you the name of the detective I work with. Or.....give my name to Amy's parents and ask them to call me directly."

Louise wasn't that easy to put off. She stayed on the phone, demanding to know why I wouldn't talk to her about what I thought. I said to her,

"There is no point in me discussing any of this with you. What is there to be gained by my surmising with you? You can't do anything with it, can you? Please just do what I said and I will help all I can."

The next day I went out to my driveway to pick up my newspaper, and read "Body of Amy Hoffman found in a water tank in a wooded area of Randolph." As I read the account it went on to say the body was fully clothed and there was no indication of rape or any marks on the body. Why are they lying? How strange, what's the point? She's already dead, what would be gained by saying it differently?

That afternoon Detective Bill Hughes from the Mount Olive precinct knocked on my door. He was a huge man, about 6' 5" tall, and good-looking. It was not uncommon for members of the local police department to stop in to see me if their rounds took them by my house.

"Bill, why are they lying about Amy Hoffman in the newspaper? I know she was naked, tortured and raped."

He simply said. "Oh." He stayed for a few minutes and left. About an hour and a half later there was another knock on my door. I opened the door, and there was Bill again only he was not alone.

"Nancy, this is Tim, he's the captain of homicide. Would you repeat to him what you told me about the Hoffman girl?"

I repeated everything I had told Bill earlier. He asked me if I knew anything else.

"Yes, a lot more, only I need to feel closer to the scene."

The three of us piled into an unmarked car and off we went. Driving through a residential section in Randolph, we passed acres of woods. The color of autumn was still lingering on some trees. Suddenly I felt ice cold.

"It's down that road."

They turned where I pointed, both of them dead quiet. A hush came over us as we entered a wooded area that opened up into an odd space. In the center of it was a water tank. In a trance I walked near the tank and went down on my knees pleading and crying for my life. The knife is used to taunt and to kill.

Looking in the killer's face, I drew his image in my mind. A flood of thoughts poured through as Amy flew into the light and I took back my body.

Back in the car, images continued to flip into view and there was no escape. A foggy evening, dusky images of a slim, dark-haired man who grabbed Amy at knifepoint as she sat in her open car. His blue car was right next to hers.

Not knowing why, but trusting my intuition, I turned to Bill:

"Drive to the next town."

We were in Chester now driving towards Mendham. Pointing to the police station, I asked to go in. I still didn't consciously have a clue as to what I was doing. Bill and Tim introduced me to the captain.

"Listen to her, she is psychic, we vouch for her."

"You have an officer whose last name begins with C."

"I've got two."

"Not the soft C, the hard C."

"Oh, you mean Coleman?"

"Yes. He gave three motor vehicle tickets this summer to a man who came up from Florida. He used to live in Hackettstown. Now he lives in The Hollow in Morristown. He murdered at least two people in Florida and was wrongly released from jail. His first name is James, his last name is K.... itch, something long and Polish sounding. I cannot pronounce it. He's moderately tall, about 5'10", he's slim, he has dark hair, he's well known to you. He or his brother worked or works at a gas station. He's got blood stains and hair in his car and he has not cleaned it."

The captain asked, "Are you serious?"

"Absolutely. You will have positive proof that he killed Amy Hoffman. He's got family up here and he is well known as a very dangerous person. He's committed multiple murders. This is a serial killer. He will kill again unless you stop him now."

The captain thanked me for my information, and Tim and Bill left with me. We went back towards my house, talking, and very excited that we had something to go on. All the while, I kept seeing James. I could see his face, I could see his eyes, I could describe his house. Not knowing what else to do we decided to go to The Hollow. The Hollow is the an area that is a gully, between two hills in Morristown, where James lived. When we arrived at The Hollow, we started driving around.

"It's a white narrow house next to a yellow one."

I didn't know what street it was on, so we kept driving around, just looking. It came to me at that point that either James or his brother worked at a gas station, and he had access to several different cars. They asked which car was used in the murder, and I could not name the model, but was able to describe the car. I proceeded to describe a blue/green car.

Weeks went by and Tim, Bill and I were in contact by phone daily. Tim was in charge of homicide, and we were all wondering why we hadn't heard anything yet. Meanwhile, the prosecutor's office had a man in charge who was the prime investigator for the county. I was devastated. I had no clue as to what was going on. It was very confusing. Then I felt the murderer, James K_____,was doing it again. I could feel it building. He was going to kill again if he was not stopped.

I called Bill. "He's coming out again to kill. I can't stand this."

Each day I became more and more anxious. My dreams were filled with snakes and knives. Wednesday evening Bill called:

"A woman just died. She was thrown out of a car on Route 80 at a rest area. Can you come with us?"

When I arrived they asked me what I saw. I showed them where a trucker was parked. I pointed to the entrance area:

"It's him again, I see the same car. He threw her out of the car and a trucker picked her up. She died in the trucker's arms.

"Yes." Apparently they already knew.

"She was driving on Washington Valley Road outside of Morristown, and she was run off the road by James' car."

Deidre O'Brien, the woman who just died, was one more victim in his line of fire.

"We are not on the case anymore. All information is to be turned over to the prosecutor's office for investigation."

Tim's statement left us in limbo. I couldn't leave it alone. Finally, one night I called Dr. Williams.

"You are a hypnotherapist, aren't you?"

"Yes."

I told him about the case. "I need to undergo hypnosis and see if I can retrieve more information or find out if I'm mistaken. Bill Hughes is a detective, he will be with me and we will tape the session."

We agreed to meet at his home a few nights later. Bill and I were greeted by a noisy terrier. He would not stop barking. Louise had to take him to another part of their home, while George, Bill and I went into the living room to begin the hypnotherapy. I sat in a big comfortable chair and began to listen to George's soothing voice as he started to hypnotize me. He instructed me to go back to the person who was committing all these murders. The next thing I knew, I am watching a scene. I started to describe it to George and Bill. "I see a small brown car with a hatchback. In the car I see a man who is extremely wild looking. Frightening looking. If it is James, it's a much bigger version of him. It's not him, it's a big man with lots of hair. James did not have lots of hair. And he is very broad, unlike James. I see a woman with pigtails, sitting there terrified. The next thing I see as the car pulls up to an intersection, is the woman running out of the car and losing a shoe. She runs to the car behind them and the driver of that car gets out to help her, but the man from the brown hatchback gets out with a knife and goes towards the other man and says, "Get out of here!". The man from the second car jumped back into his car and pulls away as fast as he can. Now the only thing I see is an American flag. I pulled myself out of the hypnotic state at this point because I couldn't stand it anymore. It was horrible. I did not understand what I was seeing. This man may have been James, but he seemed much larger and more terrorizing than my previous images. I did not understand what was going on.

I got home at about 8:15 PM, exhausted and anxious to lie in bed and read. I got into a set of oversized floppy pajamas, and climbed into bed. As I was getting into bed, the phone rang. It was Bill.

"I'm picking you up," he said.

"What?"

"Abduction on American Road in Morris Plain."

I realized what the American flag in my vision meant. "I'll be ready."

I was dressed in a minute, and walking out the door as Bill pulled up. I got in the car, and we picked up Tim. We went into the Morris Plain precinct and Bill told the prosecutor, "I have Nancy Fuchs with me." He said, "Get her out of here. I don't believe in her!." Bill and Tim snuck me out the back way. There were TV and newspaper reporters in the front and we wanted to avoid them. They did, however, report the next day that a "secret witness woman" was rushed out the back door.

We spent until about five or six AM driving all over searching for these people. Exactly what I had seen in my vision was reported to the police by the man who tried to help the abducted woman who attempted to flee from the brown hatchback. He had come running into the Morris Plain police department yelling about the man with the knife and the brown hatchback. They went to American Road where they found a woman's shoe. They never found her, they never found him. There was no report of a missing woman. We have no clues.

I searched with Bill and Tim all night. I ended up with a 105 degree fever. I was hysterical. I had never seen so many police helicopters in the air or police cars on the road as I had on that night. They came from every surrounding county and some were even from Pennsylvania. They sealed off every road in the area, but he was gone. He was probably parked right under their noses somewhere, and was most likely at home with her, killing her. We have no idea. After that I thought, "I don't know what's going on."

A few weeks after Deidre's death I was again feeling anxious. The fear that James was coming out again prevailed. Since 1975 I held a Thursday evening class in my home, where we meditated, studied a spiritual issue and did metaphysical exercises. I had a group of people I knew very well coming to class that night. I told them about what had been going on, and that it was totally confidential, not to be discussed outside of the room. I told them I was very confused about what was going on.

We all joined hands and I spoke out loud to God that if it does not interfere in any sense, and if it is within the murderer's spiritual path, I am asking that he please feel the pain that he refuses to feel himself, particularly the pain he keeps giving to women. Bring back to him, God, the mirror of his own feelings and have him feel it all himself, and make him come forward. I call it mind mirror work.

The next morning Tim called me and said, "What did you do, Nancy?" I told him what I had done in class, calling on God to make this murderer feel his own feelings, and maybe turn himself in. I wanted to know what happened and asked Tim to explain. He told me that a man had called for an ambulance, and claimed he had been stabbed by a dark haired woman who ran him off the road. The ambulance was sent, and the police were called in. They proceeded to come to his car, where he was, and found he had knife wounds, which they later realized were self inflicted. When the police looked over the car they also realized it was a very similar car to the one I had described. He was taken in for questioning, and put into custody. They obtained a warrant to search the car, and sure enough, they found Amy Hoffman's hair and blood inside. He was convicted of murder, and his name was James Koedatich. The one thing that I saw also throughout the whole thing which was very peculiar, was that James always had a long mop of hair in my visions, except every time I would work with my vision for a few minutes, he would lift it to reveal very short hair with a high widow's peak. It turned out that when he was brought to jail, he shaved off all his hair, but left a high widow's peak.

(For Bill Hughes' recounting of this story and of how he became a believer, see Appendix G).

PHONE 201-475-6361

OFFICE OF THE COUNTY PROSECUTOR
WARREN COUNTY
COURT HOUSE
BELVIDERE, NEW JERSEY 07823

PROSECUTOR
HOWARD A. McGINN

FIRST ASSISTANT PROSECUTOR
ROBERT J. ELLWOOD, JR.

ASSISTANT PROSECUTORS
FRANK J. BUCSI
WILLIAM M. McCURLEY

CHIEF INVESTIGATOR
DANIEL H. GARDNER

INVESTIGATORS
KENT BERGMANN
ANTHONY A. BUCAREY
RALPH ROHRBACH

August 2, 1982

Nancy Fuchs
Wildwood Avenue
Budd Lake, New Jersey

Dear Ms. Fuchs:

This is to advise you of an investigation being conducted by the
Blairstown Township Police Department and the Warren County Prosecutors
Office.

On July 15, 1982, the body of a young female was discovered in Cedar
Ridge Cemetary, Blairstown Township. As of this time the person whose
body was found has not been identified. After exhausting those leads
available to the investigating authorities, a suggestion to use your
abilities and services was made. The investigators involved are in
agreement and respectfully request your cooperation in this investigation.

Please contact this undersigned to arrange for a mutually convienient
time for you to examine the crime scene and evidence available.

Thanking you in advance for your anticipated cooperation in this matter.

Respectfully,

Kent Bergmann
Lieutenant

KB:ml

LETTER FROM THE WARREN COUNTY
PROSECUTOR'S OFFICE

CHAPTER SIXTEEN
UNSOLVED MURDER

"Mom, it's Ross English," Rebecca called out from the kitchen.

Walking into my bedroom I wondered what was going on in town that he would be calling about. I didn't feel anything significant locally. She hung up as Ross began telling me:

"I just got a call from Warren County's Detective Bureau. Lt. Joseph (not his real name) is a friend, we go way back. He's heard we've worked together on a few things and knew I could reach out to you. Remember reading about a girl's body found in Washington Township a few months ago?"

"No, but you know I don't read newspapers, I don't watch TV and I absolutely avoid conversations about that stuff. If I'm going to work on something I'd rather go in cold."

"I told Joseph that. He's hoping you would help him on that case. They have reached a dead end. You interested?"

"Sure, tell him I'll do whatever I can."

Lt. Joseph called a few hours later. Pleasant sounding man, not tough at all. Warm and friendly. Yet I could feel a determination and dedication coming through beyond many I had met. He gave me directions and I gulped, an hour each way. No pay offered and I would be paying for my own transportation. My poor wagon. It had over 120,000 miles and I prayed over every trip it made, thanking it again and again for getting my family safely from one place to another. Actually in the seven years of ownership it had only failed me twice. Both times were in driveways while visiting two of my closest friends. One was able to repair it himself and the other called her repairman who arrived and fixed it while we played backgammon. Not bad for an old Chevy wagon. I don't know whether it's the light I place around it or that I lucked into a great car. Either way I was able to relax as I drove out to see Lt. Joseph the next week.

Although their police station was in a rural area it had all the finesse that ours didn't. It was a large stone building in the center of town. The town was only a four block radius, so it was easy to find. The lawn around it was immaculate. Everything appeared clean, neat and orderly. Until I got to the detective bureau. I don't know what it is with them, the intensity of the job, the high from the donuts and coffee, but I've never seen an orderly office.

"You must be Nancy Fuchs. Hello, I'm Lt. Joseph."

His warm handshake matched his voice. Not much taller than me, I'm 5'8" so he's about 5'10." One of his blue eyes was not focusing and I never asked what that was about. Trying not to stare at it but kept wanting to catch glimpses to see if I recognized the physical problem, I never figured it out either.

"I don't know how you work," he said, "I've never done this before. Can I get you something to drink?"

"Coffee, please." Why not join them in their speed trip.

"How do you take it?"

"Light, no sugar, thanks."

Lt. Joseph motioned me to a wooden seat by his desk where I waited for his return. Chaos on his desk too. Just like mine. I always thought I could find any paper I needed and was proud of that ability. I wondered if he was like that.

"Here's your coffee. I'd like you to meeet two other detectives we will be working with. They'll be back in a few minutes. One's at the lab and the others in court."

"No hurry, I can start on my own if that's all right with you. All I want to start with is for you to confirm that this is a murder of a female. Yes?"

"Yes. I have an object that belonged to her. Would you like to see it?"

Lt. Joseph was seated at his desk. He opened a drawer and pulled out a small plastic ziplock like the jewelers use. In it was a piece of jewelry. He handed the bag to me.

"May I take it out of its bag?"

"Of course."

Opening the bag and turning it upside down into my left palm, a thin gold colored chain with a small cross lay in my hand. A dead girl's necklace. Getting my mind to stop thinking I asked, "Is there somewhere I can go to sit alone quietly?"

"Right this way."

Following Joseph I kept my eyes focused on the hall and building not letting my mind get scared of the feelings and visions starting to surface.

"Here we are."

Lt. Joseph opened the door to a small chapel. Perfect.

"Thank you, I can find my way back to you when I'm done. I won't be long."

Closing the door quietly he left me to myself. Now I can let go and work. Praying for guidance, I held the necklace still in my left hand. Slowing down my breathing and concentrating on the sound of my breath, I forgot where I was or what I was doing there.

Good. This was a perfect place to work in. "Tell me about this girl," I directed my subconscious. "Tell me about this girl." I repeated those words several times and then stayed still. Watching the dark screen that covers my mind. An image started emerging within seconds. A slightly built long haired girl was being chased in a cemetery by a very large red-haired man whom I knew to be named John. As she fell he picked up a stone and bent over. He proceeded to forcibly beat her head until there was very little left of it. I kept watching, looking for more clues to who they were and anything about him I could see. His beard, darker than his hair. Pennsylvania, he lives there. She's a runaway from a fairly okay middle class family.

Her thoughts started penetrating my mind. "Don't want my family to know what happened to me. I'm so ashamed of what I did when I ran away. Don't tell them."

"Who is them?"

"Don't tell them. I picked him up. I needed the money. I didn't know he was so bad. He's crazy. I'm terrified."

"Do you know what he did to you?"

"Yes, he raped me."

"More than that. Do you know where you are now?"

"I'm here."

"Where's here?"

"Here, with you." Trying to be gentle I went on.

"Are you sitting down next to me?"

Her voice changed, "I don't know."

"How old are you?"

"Fifteen, I ran away at 13."

"So many years on your own. That's sad. Do you remember John chasing you in the cemetery?" Suddenly the pain erupted all through me and I knew she had made the connection.

"He killed me. Oh my God, I'm dead. How can I be? I don't get it."

"We are talking mind to mind. I'm sorry, I don't know how else to help you see. I can help you adjust if you like."

"Oh God, please do something, this is horrible, all I see is that stone."

"I know, you are so traumatized that you've been stuck. I'll do what I can. What name do I call you?"

"No, no name, my parents are not going to find out. No name, please do something. How can I go on?"

My eyes still closed I called on the universe to bring a loving guide to take her across to the light. In my mind I saw a woman I had seen before. She was carrying a bouquet of flowers and she offered them to No Name. No Name took them and started to cry. The woman put her arm around No Name and led her away, down a path to a very bright light. The image stopped and I became acutely aware of the wood pew I was sitting on, sounds in the corridor and the sickening feeling of having just experienced a murder. I opened my eyes, put the necklace back in its bag and left the chapel.

Walking down the corridor I came to the same office I had entered a half hour before. So much had changed though. No longer a stranger, I felt apart of everything there and now probably as frustrated and upset as any of the folks on the case.

"Hi, I'm back." Lt. Joseph was talking with two other men seated by his desk. "This is Nancy, David Heater and Robert are the other guys on the case."

I sat in the same chair as before.

"Want me to freshen your coffee?" Robert asked.

"No thanks, I usually sip the same cup from morning all day long. Don't want too much caffeine in me. Want to hear what I saw?"

"All ears."

All three of them looked interested. I would too if I had a case like that and absolutely no evidence and no leads.

"I know she died last year, her remains are not enough for absolute identification. She was about 15 at the time of death, about 5'1", slight build and long dark hair. Her killer has killed several times. I hate to think it, but he may continue his rampage for quite awhile. She picked him up. Because of this, there is difficulty in finishing this case. She feels ashamed of her lifestyle and stuck in her shame. Even though her body is dead, her mind is continuing and she does not want anyone she once knew to know what happened to her. Her killer weighs over 220 lbs., is in his mid 30's..." I continued to relate everything I saw.

I left out the part where she and I made contact. I didn't want to lose my credibility over something I may believe can exist but they may have a hard time understanding. This wasn't the place to argue philosophy or physics.

"I don't know how you could possibly know what we know, but you do. All true, except of course the description of the killer. It may be true but we don't know."

Lt. Joseph turned to the others and waited for their response.

"What do we do next? Do you think going to the cemetery might help?" David offered.

"Couldn't hurt," was all I could say. Driving out of town, I sat in the front seat with David, while Robert and Lt. Joseph sat in the back.

"We named her Princess Doe. Don't know why but Jane Doe doesn't seem enough. We're hoping with enough press attention some more information may come up," Lt. Joseph said.

We were passing a shopping center and I asked if we could pull in.

"I want to go into the Pizza parlor."

"Sure, we could all use a drink. You hungry?" Robert asked.

"No, I think they were in there. Have you checked it out?" "No," was Lt. Joseph's reply. Walking in I slowed my walk down so I could feel the imprint of past energy lingering in the parlor. I stared in the air. Slow haze appeared and then I saw them, briefly, less than a second, then it was gone. They had been here the day of the murder.

"Done. Got what I need." They were ordering drinks when I spoke. I walked outside, I needed different air. They followed me.

"Come up with anything?" Robert said as he walked me to the front door of the car.

"Not much, just that they were in there that day."

"We can question them later," David said as he took his notebook out and wrote in it.

We drove out of the parking lot of the shopping mall, made a left to head further west and I turned my head to the right. A group of stones caught my eye, all in a row... a cemetery. The pizza parlor was less than a block from the cemetery. They surely were there. How horrible, one minute pizza, next, terror and death. What a sick world. Sure enough David pulled up by the cemetery. It was definitely the one I had seen in my vision.

"Just let me walk around by myself." I didn't want any interfering thoughts, and I hate preconceived notions of what happened, they're usually wrong. If I'm going to find out anything I have to keep an empty mind and let the truth pour through.

As I walked around the cemetery I suddenly felt scared of a clump of trees in a far corner, away from the road. Walking over to it I felt like running far away but instead I got firmer and more determined with each step. Can't believe how frightening just the leftover energy can be. There it is, the same image, only this time I'm looking up at a face. His scar, on his right cheek. It's staring at me/her, this thing that is taking pleasure in my/her pain. My head...couldn't take the pain. I hurriedly walked over to the three guys. They felt like home.. safe, secure. When detectives, who reek of the negativity and pain they are constantly exposed to, feel comfortable to hang out with, I'm in trouble. Most detectives start turning cold early.

"Not getting much. He chased her back to those trees. Only other thing I can make out is a scar on his cheek. It's deep, you can't miss it."

The rest of our conversation was a repeat of earlier ones, going over and over every detail in case we missed something. Heading back I realized I still had another hour's drive ahead of me. My whole body joined my mind in exhaustion. I hardly spoke to them and they seemed lost in their own troubled thoughts. Saying goodbye at their parking lot I was grateful to slide into my wagon and be alone.

All the way home I kept seeing his face, his eyes filled with a strange longing. The closest translation of that longing I could come up with was a longing to never be forgotten, to own another soul, to insure the memory of their own existence at any cost and above that, a pleasure at delivering pain, as if that brought him power. With every blow he felt more and more alive. Shaking my head to move my thoughts, I put my radio on to a lively rock station.

Fortunately it was a song I knew. Joining my voice to the song, I started a new rhythm in my mind, letting the past recede as I grabbed hold of a different feeling through the lyrics. By the time I reached home the visions were vague enough that they were no longer interfering with my ability to function. Absolutely nothing came of that day's information. Lt. Joseph kept in touch, hoping I'd deliver some more precise clues but I didn't. The case remained unsolved and open as it still does.

(For further recountings of David Heater on the Princess Doe case, see Appendix H).

Psychic's vision keeps turning heads

Denville Township resident puts abilities to a variety of good uses

By MAUREEN SALAMON
Daily Record

DENVILLE TWP. — To Nancy Fuchs Weber, developing psychic power is much like learning how to play the piano.

Everyone has the ability to do either, she says, but "not everyone is a Beethoven."

The Denville wife and mother says she has had a lifelong ability to foresee the future and to mentally replay events she did not witness.

She has used her power in diverse ways, from healing her own back injury and leading stress reduction seminars to working as a psychic detective. Weber has helped several Morris County police departments solve a host of crimes, including rape, kidnapping and murder.

She was there when police needed help cracking the State Trooper Philip Lamonaco murder in 1981, when James Koedatich was on the loose after murdering Amie Hoffman in 1982 and when Michael Manfredonia killed Long Valley teen Rachel Domas in 1985. All were convicted.

Today, she is working with a New York reporter to uncover the identity of the Zodiac killer.

Weber's ability to predict death has turned heads since she was a little girl, but not in a favorable way. She learned about rejection and loneliness from those who shunned her visions.

Knew early

"Early in life, I would know things about people's lives that were secrets. I thought everyone knew," she said. "I would tell people world and personal events yet to come. The looks on other people's faces made it very clear to me that I was unique and that I made them uncomfortable."

But despite her early uneasiness with her ability, her visions "just happened," she said. In her 20s, she used her psychic powers "to help save lives, to diagnose difficult cases for doctors and to find things."

Later, she came to terms with her ability after she healed her own crippling injury. As a registered nurse, Weber was thrown to the ground one day by a 300-pound patient. A nerve in her leg and several discs in her spine were crushed.

Doctors predicted life in a wheelchair for her by her mid-30s, but she "blew them all away" by taking another psychic's advice to heal herself by placing her hands on herself and asking God to take

IVAN SAPERSTEIN / Special to the Daily Record
Psychic Nancy Fuchs Weber says she has had a lifelong ability to foresee the future and recall events she did not witness.

the pain away.

"I took my brace off, took karate classes and danced for the first time in years," Weber said. "It forced me to perceive the world differently.

"As a nurse, I knew the physical condition of my system. I knew that physiology and psychology were linked. But the spiritual powers that exist were not anything I considered before.

"It wasn't until after the healing that my visions ... led me to work with anyone and everyone who needed my assistance," she said. "One of my rules is that I don't go looking for work. It looks for me, and then I know it's appropriate."

Detective work came looking for Weber in 1981 after she moved to the state from New York. Mount Olive police found out about her after one of their officers met her grade-school son during a visit to his school. Soon after she was asked to work on a rape case.

The force gave her a special police officer's badge for her work.

More honors

Other honors followed, including a county Sheriff's Department commendation for helping to locate three young children who were abducted by their father and taken to California.

Still later, by going to murder sites, looking at photos or just thinking things out, Weber helped crack some of the biggest crime cases in the history of Morris County. In fact, she said her assistance pegged the identity, whereabouts or background of many of the county's most recently convicted murderers.

Her psychic visions come to her in different ways. For instance, when trying to locate the three kidnapped children, she sat with the children's grandmother and a sheriff's officer and talked about her impressions.

Easily enough, she identified California as the state where the children's father took them. But Weber was stuck on the name of the

> 'There are a few dozen cases I know I was instrumental in solving.'
>
> Nancy Fuchs Weber,
> Denville psychic

town until her dog, Ramona, barked.

The town was Ramona, Calif.

"It took a few months, but they were reunited," she said.

Except in special circumstances, Weber no longer uses her talents for local police departments. After working on several hundred cases, she quit last year, frustrated by what she called the "big egos" of some officials.

In some instances, she said police denied her involvement in cases in which she said she played a big role.

"There are a few dozen cases I know I was instrumental in solving," she said. "I'm asked to participate and review police records and I'm not even acknowledged. It's frustrating."

Busy writing

While she is now working with a New York reporter to solve the city's Zodiac killer mystery, Weber busies herself mostly by writing books, conducting workshops and giving speeches.

A blend of actual and fictional cases of serial killers will be employed in her book "We All Must Die Sometime," while a compilation of the cases she has solved as a psychic detective will be chronicled in a second book.

"I prefer at this point of my life to do more lecturing and writing," Weber said. "I feel my hands are full."

Weber will deliver a lecture titled "The Psychic in You" at the Dover Masonic Temple at 8 p.m. on Aug. 7. Admission is $5 for members of the Association for Higher Awareness and $6 for non-members.

Reprinted with permission from the Daily Record

MORRIS COUNTY DAILY RECORD
AUGUST 1, 1990

CHAPTER SEVENTEEN
IS HE A SERIAL KILLER?

Walking into the bedroom, there was no escaping the sight that waited. I walked to the left side and stared at the blood all over the wall by the head of the bed. Her blood, none of it his. He left her none. The sheets were covered with blood, I kept staring, hoping to remove myself from the present horror and back into the real one where it came from. Then I saw it. She was tied to the bed, wrists tied behind her, mouth covered with tape. He had a hammer in his hand, and he repeatedly brought it down on her head. Enough, I couldn't look anymore. I walked around to the other side, "I think I've seen enough. Let's go somewhere else. "

David Heater and Robert must have known what I was going through, after all they had feelings also, and no one except a killer walks out easily on that. Sitting in the same office I had sat in 5 years before, coffee in hand, I began, "I saw a red -haired, bearded guy, name's John, scar on cheek, overweight, bulky, large western belt buckle, always in dungarees."

It had all started with a woman named Judith. She booked an appointment at my office for a session. Opening the door I greeted Judith, walked her downstairs to the living/waiting room, showed her where the bathroom was and went upstairs to get her a glass of water. She seemed inordinately sad, a great deal of grief was covering her. Her eyes told me she could not live well with a past deed and was here to change it. I brought her the water and we went into my office.

This office was soft gray and pale blue. Very soothing with two overstuffed chairs. I like to kick my shoes off when I work, it's like rolling up my sleeves to get ready for hard work. Shoes at the side of my chair I was braced for the worst. Here sat a sweet looking woman who by the condition of her hands and general appearance seemed to work hard for a living. Her hair slightly unkempt, she wore it in two braids, her general look was exhausted by life. I took a deep breath and plunged right in.

"You had a tragedy in the family. Your cousin died recently?" was my first question.

Tears and a nod said enough.

"She was murdered?" Another nod.

As I spoke a sequence of images came to me, too brutal to share. I saw a man beating a woman tied to a bed. There were details to the image that were so difficult to keep because I had all I could do not to let Judith see my reaction. She didn't need any more upset.

"Your cousin worked in a hospital, hard worker, drank too much, but in general was kind and loving. She had a boyfriend who really cared. He is a sweet man and is devastated. He is a suspect, but Judith, I don't think he is involved at all. The cops on the case are looking at the men in her life and it isn't them. It's not a crime of passion or anything of that sort at all. This is a serial killer."

I had said all I wanted her to know.

"Would you be willing to talk to the detectives who are working on the case?"

Judith's voice was slightly hoarse. Cigarettes and recent crying had done that . "Just give them the information and tell them to call Detective Lt. Ross English of the Mt. Olive Police Department for verification of who I am. You shouldn't have any problem. I think we'll get him Judith. It feels like he is ready to stop and be caught."

Judith didn't ask what I meant and I didn't explain. We chatted about the changes it brought in her family, her shoulders seemed a bit straighter and stronger when she left, her eyes filled with less horror, more hope. The next day David Heater called.

"Remember me?" was his opener.

"How could I forget?"

Hanging up, I realized I had just agreed to another day of work away from my kids, no pay and lots of sadness.

A few days later I was walking into Betty Kramer's apartment with Robert and David. Her apartment was on the first floor with a staircase at the entrance leading to another apartment. I looked up the stairs and shivered. Something up there was definitely disturbing. I saw a form, translucent and vague on the staircase. It was a young, very thin male, about 19 years of age. He was mentally blocking my vision of what was upstairs as if he was hiding something or someone.

Entering Betty's' apartment, it was eerie to see everything exactly as it was on her last day on earth. Walking around the living room I was taken by the beautiful shades of blue she chose for her chairs and couch. Dark but bright and comfortable. She was neat, nothing out of place. Her kitchen was small, I kept walking around it sensing another presence. Three steps and I'd turn around finding myself back at the entrance to the living room. Someone had been in the kitchen with Betty. She was getting him a drink. I didn't feel fear, but rather discomfort. She didn't like this guy, he was on the gruff side, gravelly voice and a look that said, "Who gives a damn." Yet she was friendly with him. Definitely not her type. She liked sweet men, giving and kind. She had a boyfriend who was more on the shy side, quiet and caring. No, this man felt nothing like her boyfriend.

I went into the bathroom hoping to uncover a clue. The year before I had found a bloodstain in a bathroom in an attempted murder case. It helped indict the suspect. It was his blood. Nothing here. I knew I was stalling until I could face her bedroom. That's where I would find out what happened. Time to go in. Robert and David were quietly walking behind me staying out of the way, giving me plenty of space to do whatever I do.

Now we were in their office and a guy named John was busy occupying my vision. David responded with "No such guy, what about her boyfriend, Joe? We think he did it. He was supposed to come over that night at 8:00PM and claims he was tired and didn't go there until 11:00 PM when he walked in and found her."

"Poor soul, he found her, that's awful. He's not lying, he called her to tell her he'd be late. There's probably a record of the call. He was tired, that's probably why she even let the killer in. She knew him but he was not someone close to her. Are you sure there is no one with red-hair?" I insisted.

"Well," David chimed in, "there's her upstairs neighbor, but he doesn't have a scar on his cheek and he doesn't wear western belts. At least I've never seen it."

"Go back and look. He's the one and he does have a scar on his cheek. He killed her with a hammer. Repeated blows to the head. True?"

"Yeah, there was nothing left of her skull. Could be a hammer. What about her ex.? He lives in Florida but is a strange guy with a record."

"Absolutely not, zero interest in her. Besides, he can prove where he was that night. I'm telling you go look at her neighbor. Does he have a young friend, male, about 19, living with him?" I persisted.

"Yeah, he does. Maybe we should go talk with him,"

David looked at me with a strange question in his eyes. He said, "Do you remember giving the same description for the killer of Princess Doe 5 years ago?"

"You're kidding...you know that's true. Same one, same style of murder, both women's heads crushed. I always thought he was a serial killer, but he must have moved from Pennsylvania. Please question her neighbor."

The rest of our conversation was friendly chatter while I gathered myself again for the ride home. The call came from David 2 days later, "Nancy, I don't know how you do it, but there it was, scar on his cheek, western buckle, and best of all a confession. He won't tell us where the hammer is but we have a solid case without it."

John was found guilty of first degree murder and given a life sentence. Two years later I was invited to be a guest speaker at a group dedicated to giving a voice to crime victims. I walked into a large room, it was pretty empty except for a dozen chairs in the round at the far end, near a row of windows. A group of people were standing around a table that held cups, coffee urn and cookies. I walked over and introduced myself.

"I'm Dick, the founder of Voices for Victims," said a man who looked like he was more of a fighter than a victim. Strong, talkative and opinionated, he introduced his wife and the others standing with us. We joined some newcomers in and sat in a circle.

A client of mine, Theresa, had found this group and taken to attending their meetings. Her brother had been murdered two years before and she was having panic attacks. She called me to ask if I would speak at the group and so here I was. Theresa introduced herself and everyone took their turn. Before Dick could speak he looked up, someone had walked into the room late saying, "Sorry uncle, just finished work." I looked up and there was Judith, Betty's cousin. Judith knew I was coming, it was in the announcement. "I was just introducing our guest speaker. She works with the police and counsels family members," Dick was interrupted. "Uncle, she's the woman I told you about. She found Betty's murderer." We all just looked at each other.

(For Dave Heater's further comments on this case, see Appendix H).

❧❧❧

MOUNT OLIVE CHRONICLE, THURSDAY, MAY 16, 1985

Reaching Out To Victims

Budd Lake resident Nancy Fuchs, left, discusses crime victims rights with Kathy Whalen, owner of Nature's Daughter when both participated in the recent fashion show held to help raise funds to help victims of crime. Crime Victim's Aid, a regional director of crime victims services for New York, New Jersey and Pennsylvania, is now available. Students of the Dover Business College sponsored the benefit fashion show to benefit the N.J. Council on Crime Victims.

Reprinted with permission from the Mount Olive Chronicle

MOUNT OLIVE CHRONICLE
MAY 16, 1985

CHAPTER EIGHTEEN
VOICES FOR VICTIMS

Dick Kramer, Betty Kramer's Father, Speaks:

I started Voices For Victims in 1988. This was the year after my daughter, Betty, was murdered by John Reese. The original purpose of Voices For Victims was to help the victims of crime and the families of victims deal with their grief. However, things have evolved since I first started the organization. In fact, things have evolved tremendously since then because I found out that there is more to it than just grief. Grief is only one of the problems the victims have. That particular part is the absence of any kind of knowledge or ideas about what happens in a murder case and how from the victim's standpoint it is as if they were a nuisance. Nobody pays any attention and nobody tells them everything. This is basically what I'm doing now. I'm trying to help people through that kind of thing.

I can grieve with people, I can cry with them but the most important thing, I feel, is to give them some control back in their lives because it is lost. Believe me, you have no control. Everybody is telling you what to do, or what not to do. While the case is being worked on, it seems people are told very little about it. It's all very difficult to cope with. On top of this, things are happening to people that they do not understand. For example, their memory goes. One example is that when the average victim is home, they tend to lose everything. They don't remember where they put things. This is only because their minds are so full. They have questions constantly running through their minds such as, "What if we had done this, or what if we did that? Maybe the murder or crime would not have happened."

This is a difficult question that everybody asks themselves. I imagine therapists are trained for this kind of work. I had a different kind of training though. I was there, and now I work at it. I've probably been to about fifteen trials so far to learn more and more about what is going on in the courtroom, so I can understand what is happening. Now I can understand why things work the way they do in the courtroom. The strange part is that sometimes when the victims ask me questions I suddenly find myself talking as if I were on somebody else's side. The reason for this is that when I'm doing this I am showing them how things work in the courtroom. This is what they need. After I explain this to them and they understand it, they have a little more of their control back. This way, I put their feet on the floor once. Once you get them there they begin to get a little better. Not much, but a little bit. Police officers and detectives, everybody that deals with victims, regardless of what kind of victims they are need to be able to talk to them the right way. They can be victims of murder or rape, assault, it doesn't matter. You need to be able to talk to these people and have a heart and get your message through. You can be nice to them. This way you can get through to them and they can answer your questions properly. The crime I most commonly deal with is murder. It's the one I know best, although I do get involved in other crimes. I understand homicide, but as you get known as I am now, I get calls from all kinds of people with all kinds of problems. There are rapes, incest, burglary, bank robberies, scams, etc.

When people call I don't really advise them about anything. I'm not a doctor, I'm not a professional. I don't counsel, all I do is answer their questions. This helps them understand what is going on and helps them understand that they are not going crazy. One woman called me thinking she was going crazy. I had to tell her she was not going crazy, it was just that nobody was taking the time to try to help her. I explained to her that the system was working, but she had to let it grind on at its own pace. It may take five weeks to prepare for a murder case. Then there will probably be a year and a half of pre-trial hearings. If you didn't have those pre-trial hearings the trial would probably end up taking five years.

During the pre-trial hearings all kinds of questions, motions, arguments, constitutional amendments, etc. are sorted out. This is what will make the trial move ahead more quickly. I've been on all sorts of radio and television programs, in the newspapers, and the word has spread about Voices For Victims. I get many calls from professional people such as psychologists and counselors who think it would be a good idea for the people they may be treating who were victims of crime to talk to another victim. On another level, besides giving them understanding, I can also tell them all about the court system and what to expect. Sometimes the Victim-Witness coordinators in the police departments have the victims contact me also. You never know where the next phone call is coming from.

I don't have a staff working with me. I do this alone. I keep a lot of notes and maybe one day I will put out a pamphlet with all the information I have gathered. Unfortunately, I don't have the time right now. I am kept very busy running from one case to another. Voices For Victims and Dick Kramer can be contacted at P.O.Box 970, Hackettstown, New Jersey 07840. Phone number: 908-850-9600.

APPENDIX A
RECOUNTING:
JILLIAN SPEAKS

My mother heard Nancy on WMTR and told me about her about five months after my husband, Joe, left me. Nancy had been talking about finding missing people and animals. My mother called the radio station. She was given Nancy's phone number, called her, and then I called to make an appointment. We had done everything else to find the kids. We had called their doctors and schools asking them not to send records anywhere, we had staked out Joe's old haunts, anything we could think of.

The police were not really helpful, not the ones in my area. Lou Masterbone was helpful. There was a genuine concern there and it was very obvious. He also had a big interest in child snatching. I had gone to high school with Lou and he heard about my case through a mutual friend. He worked in Morris County and they had just created a division to try to locate missing children. This was an unusual case at the time. It received much publicity on TV and radio.

I saw a show on TV about a private investigator who would locate children who were kidnapped by a parent and go and steal them back. Unfortunately most of the states at the time did not have reciprocal agreements on custody cases, and sometimes this was the only way.

But even if I managed to get my children back, nothing wouldprevent Joe from taking them again. The non-custodial parent would not even be punished.

After my first meeting with Nancy, I had to bring things to her that had belonged to the children. She told me many things. She had good news for me because sometimes she had to tell parents that they would never see their children again. She said I would but it would be a long time.

Nancy said that one child was going to get hurt and would require stitches in an emergency room. It would be a dog bite. They could see snow on the mountains, but it was warm where they were.

I worked at an insurance company at the time and had access to names of hospitals on their computers. I thought they were still somewhere in Texas. I got a printout of the names of the hospitals in the area I thought they were in, and xeroxed a flyer with a picture of the children. It was sent to every one of those hospitals.

Unfortunately, Nancy could not tell me exactly where the children were. I asked her if I could come back with Lou Masterbone another time and we did. I remember Nancy told me she saw an "E" Street. She also talked about checks his mother had written to him. The canceled checks were lying on her desk, she said. His mother's checks would be the key to finding him.

She had to go for depositions and was told she had to bring her bank account with her. Lou thought she would never bring those canceled checks, but strangely enough she did. Nancy told me she would be afraid not to. She gave my lawyer all the things she had pertaining to her account. Of course there was no address on Joe's checks except the bank's stamped on the back. We called the Ramona National Bank and told them we needed his address because there was a warrant for his arrest. The bank would not release any information to the police or my lawyer because of the Privacy Act. They called me and said they could not get it.

I called the bank and told them I was Joe, short for Josephine. In thirteen months I learned a lot. I learned that some people want to help you and some don't. I also learned that sometimes you have to lie to get the information you need. I told them I had not been receiving my bank statements and could they give me the address they were sending them to. I told them they must be going to the wrong address. They said, "Sure. 1225 "E" Street, Ramona, California." That is how we found where they had been.

Unfortunately he was gone again. Nothing really tipped him off that we had found him this time. It was just coincidence. He needed money and he left for Hawaii where he found a job. The police talked to the neighbors who said he had gone there.

I called information in Hawaii and asked if they had a listing for Joe. They said he was listed, but it was an unpublished number. At the time the FBI would not get involved.

I saw a private investigator on TV, as I mentioned before, who would go and steal your kids back for you for $10,000. I went to see him in New York City and called him several times. I told him that I had found him in Hawaii, but he had an unlisted number. Joe called me back a few hours later with Joe's address and phone number, where they kids went to school, where he worked, everything.

When that private investigator gave me the phone number in Hawaii, he told me not to call them. It would alert Joe again. But I had to. When I dialed that number, I heard my daughter, Diane's voice and hung up. I just had to know it was really them.

It took six months from when they got to Hawaii to get them back because by the time we had traced them to California, they had already been gone several months. The police out there would not respond right away since there was no cooperation between the states.

When I finally knew where the kids were living, I still had to wait a week. I could only afford a Super Saver flight that was not leaving right away. It was a very costly trip. My lawyer, however, went on a day ahead of me. I had no idea if Joe would be gone again.

When I finally saw them at the police station in Hawaii, they had no shoes on. This is because they were taken right out of the house on the spot. They didn't have time to put on their shoes. They came to me, so brown from the sun. I wanted to hide them and put them under my wing and whisk them out. I was afraid Joe's friends would be outside waiting or something. He also had a woman living with him at that point. I was afraid I'd see her too. But Nancy told me, "This is it. It's over for him, you'll have your kids." She also said that I'd get them at 4:00 p.m. under an arch. I got them at ten to four under an arch.

The police were very cooperative, and they put Joe in jail overnight. Now when I see other abusers and victimizers, I go nuts. But that is the way I survive now because I don't trust anybody anymore. I'm like a bull, fighting tooth and nail. I used to think nothing bad could happen to me, but it did. The police see things with blinders on. They only see the letter of the law. That is where they fall apart, and that is why people like me become people like me. I have had it. Everybody thinks I'm a bitch. That's my attitude. The difference is I care about myself now as well as for others. I am going to take care of myself so I can take care of the children.

My advice to other women going through something like I did is: Get a lawyer who will help you hide. A restraining order is useless. Hide until there is some sort of protection for the children. Inform the schools that the children cannot be picked up by anyone other than you. It may be hard to get a court order, though you can definitely tell this to the schools if you are the custodial parent. The school has to abide by this. This goes for other places the children go to as well, even to friends' houses. Many people are afraid to let the schools and other places know there is a problem. They may be afraid they will not be believed. The fear of disbelief can be very strong, but they should do it anyway. And letters should be sent to everyone saying there is the potential of a parental abduction and that if anything happens to the child, they will be held liable.

I would change all the laws regarding any family that has broken up. Look at each case individually instead of blanketly saying, "He's their father (or mother), he has rights." What happened to my kids was wrong. They ran, they hid, he had them in church every night. It may have hurt their ability to trust. They were taken with no explanation. They did not understand what was happening.

Nancy had told me that Joe was with a woman. And he was with that woman when I got the children and he later married her. They are living in Texas. When we divorced, Joe suddenly found God. He became a minister, not ordained, but licensed. He got involved with the 700 Club. Now he doesn't come around much. They were in my house about two years ago.

I think she bought his lingo that I was a bad person. He's very convincing. She's not a dope, but he had her convinced. I don't think she's a victim though. She knew the kids were stolen when they were in Texas, and she never called or tried to help. I think that is a bit strange.

Visitation should be supervised. It should be at an agency, for example a battered wives' shelter, or they can do what we finally did after I got the children back. We hired an off duty police officer

(Joe did not know that he was an officer) to go along on all of their outings. Joe's lawyer fought hard for visitation rights. He was allowed to see the children one day a year. He had gone back to live in Texas. What he had to do was come to New Jersey the day before and go to court to arrange the visitation. He has to do this every time. It seemed as though the courts thought the piece of paper he got should make me just totally believe that he would really bring the kids back. This is why we hired the off duty police officer to tag along with them. Joe did not like that one bit.

He had to be very careful about what he said to the kids. While they were away, Joe always told the kids that I was evil, the devil had me, I was in a mental hospital, all sorts of things. I was really scared while they were out of my sight. Joe had taken the children for spite, not because he loved them. I was afraid somehow he would slip out of this guy's sight and do it again to hurt me. Fortunately, I always had a great relationship with my children and they didn't really absorb the bad things he had said about me. We were always very open. Diane was the oldest and she told me she always knew I'd be able to find them.

❧❧❧ ❧❧❧ ❧❧❧

APPENDIX B
RECOUNTING:
LOU MASTERBONE SPEAKS

As I remember it, my first encounter with Nancy was in 1980 when I got involved with Jillian on a missing persons case. Her three children had been kidnapped by her former husband, Joe. I had been following every lead possible, and kept trying and trying, but had no luck. This kidnapping occurred before there were no central computers for missing children. Finding children was much more difficult in those days.

One day, in desperation, Jillian said to me, "I want you to go to a psychic." I laughed at her, not thinking she was serious, but she insisted. At that point I figured that we had tried everything else, so why not. I thought at least it would make Jillian feel a little better. I was very concerned about her and the horrible ordeal she was going through. Jillian and I knew each other from way back, we had gone to high school together. Jillian had been to Nancy once already and gave me her name. You could definitely say I was very skeptical. I called two other police officers, Bill Hughes and Ross English, for references. They had worked with Nancy previously and told me she was good.

We went to Nancy's house in Mt. Olive, New Jersey. Her office and "reading room" was on the third floor. As we went upstairs, I still did not believe in all this. I was only there because Jillian needed support. We worked about three hours that night. The first thing Nancy felt was that Joe was in Texas with the children. She went and got an encyclopedia because she couldn't see a town. She opened to a map and pointed to Uliss, Texas. I told Nancy he had been there. We had tracked him and the children to Texas through the school records. Unfortunately, by the time we tracked him, he had already left. We had no idea where he was at this point.

One thing Nancy kept seeing was that the children's shoes were too tight, they were undernourished and their clothes didn't fit. One child, she went on to say, had stitches in her upper lip, but this was from a dog bite, not something her father did to her. This, by the way, is the exact condition they were in when we finally found them.

Nancy insisted that Joe's mother knew where he was. She would be found to have canceled checks she had made out to him and other bank records would prove she had been sending him money. Nancy said the checks were on his mother's desk in her home in New Jersey. We checked with the bank and traced Joe to California, but we did not find out exactly where he had been living.

We went back to Nancy and this is something I will never forget. She told me that they were living on a dirt road called "E" Street, or something starting with an "E". Nancy couldn't quite make out the name of the town. She had a dog named Ramona lying by her feet at the time, and when Nancy looked down at the dog, she said "Ramona, that's it! Ramona, California!".

We phoned the San Diego Police Department, the closest one to Ramona, and found he was living on a dirt road called "E" street in Ramona. We sent the police out there, but found we had missed them by twenty-four hours. They had moved on again, this time to Honolulu. The police obtained this information by questioning the neighbors.

Joe was located in Honolulu through a printing business he owned. A warrant was issued for his extradition back to New Jersey. He was arrested and the children were put in a home until Jillian could get to Hawaii. She met the children in the police station and then flew home with them.

This was one of the first child snatching cases in New Jersey, and really was in a way, a test case. There was so much publicity on this case. I can remember the show *That's Incredible* calling us for an interview. Jillian did not want to go public with the story. She thought her kids had already been through too much. In the end, because the cost of extradition and prosecution was prohibitive, the charges against Joe were dropped. All Jillian wanted was to have her children back. She had been without them for fourteen months, and thanks to Nancy we found them.

At first I did not believe in Nancy's abilities, but the turning point came when she told us about the children being in Texas. She had not had any access to the police files and she had not been told anything about Texas.

It was a strange case. We always were one-step behind Joe and the kids. Every time we would get to where we tracked them, they would be gone. In retrospect I believe that he was trying to get caught at the end. Maybe the kids were becoming too cumbersome.

If this should happen to anyone else, the first thing they should do is go to the police. They should try to find a cop that cares and is compassionate. If there is a problem finding one at the local police station, go up the ladder to the county prosecutor's office and try again. The next step is to make sure the child is entered into the central computer for missing persons within 24 hours. Then you need a lot of perseverance, perseverance, perseverance.

Today things have changed in the way child snatching is handled. Today things are handled very quickly and efficiently. There are a lot more resources available. The success rate nowadays is a lot higher than it was at the time Jillian's children were kidnapped.

APPENDIX C
RECOUNTING:
ROSS ENGLISH SPEAKS

About the burglary case, I assigned others to it as I was involved with a bigger case at the time. However it became a well known case within the department because of the results. I remember Nancy called and told me she knew who did it and where the gun was. It was a 22 rifle and Nancy told me the boy had taken it and put it in his mother's attic. Unbeknownst to his family he hid it in his mother's apartment. We questioned him with his mother present. I confronted him with the fact that there was an eyewitness. Knowing full well I was using your psychic powers as an eyewitness to it. It's not trickery. I just wanted to see what he had to say. He denied it I think, at first. He confessed when I told him the gun was in the attic. We had search warrants drawn and we recovered the rifle. Nancy also told us where the watch was. On the dresser of the other guy's girlfriend. At that point within the department there was a lot of talk of myself and Detective Poole (not his real name) and what we were able to do with what she said. Everybody was amazed. We supported the idea that we did what we did. Police have a right, when they question suspects, to say that they were seen or they have latent fingerprints to trick people into saying they did it, not lying, just getting them to say the truth. There is no reason to admit it if they think you have nothing on them.

And, after we obtained the confessions, the fingerprint on the lamp Nancy brought in, nice and clean, proved the case as well. Both men were given a jail sentence which they served.

Some of the guys didn't believe what happened, some thought we were crazy or Nancy was. There was chaos and confusion, a lot of the guys didn't know what to think about how the case was solved.

Detective Poole and I became believers after we talked to Nancy about the murder case of a young retarded woman. We could confirm some of the information she gave us from the file. The file had been in Poole's and my custody for a year and a half and no one else had access to it. It was given to me when I took over the detective bureau. It was about 8 years old and Nancy wasn't even living in New Jersey at the time of its occurrence. Nancy described in great detail and accuracy the interior of the home the woman lived in, the distance from her house to the nearby lake. I was convinced then. I was excited. The old adrenaline started to run. I'm an investigator. I'm saying to myself I need every tool I can get. I said to myself I want to pursue this. As far as we were concerned we had to believe. It was the rational thing to do.

Another amazing incident that the entire force still talks about is when Nancy called me about the bug found in the Captain's office. She called to tell me this within hours of our discovery of the object. We were keeping it a secret, concerned about the significance of the bug. She had no way of finding out except through her powers.

I came over with the troops. The Chief and the rest of the top guys. We brought over a bunch of photos of all the cops and Nancy picked out Giella right away. She said he is going to be very serious trouble, he is trouble, there is something going on. She even said he should be under suspicion for planting the bug. She was upset and told us he would blow up the town if he could.

She also pointed out a guy name Donnie. She thought he was a possible arsonist. Donnie's house had burnt down that year but they found nothing conclusive.

We, the police, found the bug and knew it was from Radio Shack but there were so many stores, I was exhausted from seeking. Nancy held up the bug and stated the date of purchase and which store it was bought in. We went the next day and there was the receipt for that particular bug on the exact date Nancy told us, September 11. It was made out to a guy she traced as working for another town. The Chief was so impressed he asked Nancy to be an auxiliary officer and gave her a badge.

Interestingly, the guy who purchased the bug lived in the same town as Giella, and he could have purchased it for him.

Within the year, Nancy was asked to return her badge and I was demoted, along with another officer. The Chief was under investigation for theft from the Attorney General's office. He believed that Nancy, another officer and myself had known of his criminal activities through Nancy's gifts. He was forced to resign.

There were two other young guys who worked with Giella and left. The county prosecutor got in touch with me because they felt I was the only credible person in the department whom they could trust for internal investigations. They introduced me to the sergeant in charge of their official corruption unit. They had a suspicion that something was going on with Giella. They had someone who saw him take pieces of a gun in the evidence room and put it in a paper bag and took it home. The prosecutor's office was after Giella because of a previous time he was involved in a bribery. They went to a jury trial and Giella won it. The prosecutor felt he was still dirty and had to be eliminated as a police officer. However, I was introduced with a Detective Jones (not a real name)and the prosecutor's office told our interim Chief that I was to work with Jones in regard to some other problems in the department. Then I was told that the new Chief wasn't to be trusted. He was eventually removed and I was put back in as a detective. At that point Giella was the target. There was now a new acting chief and I was also assigned to work with a federal agent from the ATF (Alcohol, Tobacco and Firearms) on Giella."

Before the raid of his house, Jones and I conducted an investigation. I wore two body tapes, we did an inventory of the evidence room. We found many parts and guns missing. It was to the point where he was under total suspicion. Then I had Giella do an inventory with me. When I asked him to show me certain weapons and he wouldn't, I said "Hold it up. That's just a skeleton of it, where's the rest of it?" He said, "I don't know". So I asked, "What happened to these?"And Giella says, "I don't know." I said, "You and I are the only two who have keys to it and you're the evidence custodian. As far as I'm concerned, I didn't take them. Where the hell are they?" His answer was, "I don't know." At that point the prosecutor's office walked in, identified themselves, read him his rights and let him call his lawyer. At that point he was taken to his house and a search warrant was executed. Well, the investigation went on from there. That's when I called Nancy and informed her that everything she said was coming true."

She then told me there were barrels of explosives. We got another search warrant and went back in and found them. Explosive powder. He was allowed to have some because he made reloads. A factory load 38 or 357 bullet or 45. After it's fired with the lid it can be reloaded by putting a new primer in, filling it with gun powder and putting a wad cutter in. It's different than the actual round ball bullet. It's a piece of lead and they're used in practice. He had more than he was allowed. He was indicted. He then turned states' evidence against many. It led to many arrests. They were satisfied that he had earned his non-prison custodial sentence. He had pleaded guilty to one count of official misconduct, we had 152 counts against him. He was sentenced to 5 years in jail and a ten thousand dollar fine. The five years were suspended. He moved his family out of the state, paid the fine, and flew out himself that very same day to join them..

Jones became the new Chief. He recently advised me that he received a call from the ATF that Giella was arrested for possession of explosives, stolen, I believe, from a national guard armory. He was in the process of selling them to mercenaries. He wasn't willing to talk about the details and the rest of his official misconduct on record from Mt. Olive Township. Chief Jones and I volunteered to go down to the state where Giella was living and fill them in. Apparently that became unnecessary when it was mentioned to Giella that we would. We haven't heard from them since. He is either in prison or facing prison right now. He has a mind of a criminal as far as I am concerned.

❧❧❧

APPENDIX D
RECOUNTING:
SUE PARTHEMUS SPEAKS

My German Shepherd, Bunny, was in my car when it was stolen on a Tuesday evening in October, 1982, in Ellicott City, Maryland.

I placed an ad in the Baltimore Sun, offering a $500.00 reward for Bunny's return. A woman named Denise saw the ad and called me. She was from Towson, Maryland. She told me about a psychic from New Jersey who was very good at locating missing animals. She gave me Nancy's name and phone number and I called her.

When Nancy answered, I explained my problem to her. Right away she said, "Your dog is in Virginia". I told her that was impossible. She said that is what she saw psychically, but I should send her a photo of Bunny, and she could try to get an image from that. I sent a photo out to her immediately.

A few days later Nancy called me back. She had received Bunny's photograph, and still insisted the dog was in Virginia. I once again could not believe this, that someone would be able to drive my 13 year old station wagon that far, or that someone would travel that distance with such an old dog. Bunny was 12 years old at the time. Nancy said she would not be able to work with me unless I was more open minded and could accept the possibility that Bunny was where she said she was. I had been thinking very negatively about the possibility of her finding Bunny. I was setting up a sort of mental barrier. I was willing to do anything to find my pet, and was able to change my attitude enough, I suppose, because Nancy did start to see more clearly where Bunny might be.

Nancy told me she was seeing water and the mountains. She also saw railroad tracks. She told me that in my search later in the day I would come across a green pick-up truck with wooden slats and a bandanna lying on the front seat, but would not find Bunny there. I was amazed later when I actually did walk by the truck Nancy described. The truck really had no significance in our search, but it did serve to give me faith in Nancy's abilities. We did not find the dog that day, and when I spoke to Nancy later she said that I was looking in all the wrong places. Much to my amazement she then told me the dog was in Harpers Ferry, West Virginia, quite a long way from where I lived.

Nancy once again described a scene in the mountains, with a river and railroad tracks. She said that Bunny was safe, and that I should mentally wrap my love around her. She predicted that Bunny would be returned to me and would be unharmed.

Interestingly enough, three other psychics had seen my ad in the paper and contacted me. They also said that Bunny would be returned to me, and saw mountains and water, but could not give me a specific place to look for her.

I headed for Harpers Ferry as soon as Nancy gave me this clue. I was using cabdrivers in my search, hoping that maybe one of them had seen my dog somewhere. They also knew where kids tend to take cars when they steal them and are done joy riding.

When I was riding in one of the cabs on the outskirts of Harpers Ferry, I suddenly had an overwhelming feeling that we should turn left. We went to the top of a hill and I started calling out Bunny's name. There was a house on this hill and a woman came out and said, "What do you want?". I said, "I want my dog!". She said, "Your dog is in Harpers Ferry." I immediately called my brother to help in the search.

We went to a place in the mountains around Harpers Ferry called Hobo Village, where it is known that criminals sometimes hide out. It was a terribly filthy place, with trash everywhere. We had a picture of Bunny, and took it door to door until we came upon a woman who had seen my dog.

"That dog's been down at the bottom of the mountain, crying for two weeks," the woman told me. The man who stole Bunny had apparently removed her collar and leash and left her by the railroad tracks. Bunny would not leave the collar and leash .... they must have been her security. She only left the spot temporarily to eat a few scraps of food this woman had offered her. After eating, Bunny would go back to her collar and leash and cry. This is where we finally found her. She was filthy and exhausted, but in pretty good condition, considering what she had been through.

Bunny's story made national headlines. As it turned out the FBI and Secret Service had even gotten involved because my car ended up being used in a homicide before it was finally abandoned. I had hundreds of calls from wonderful caring people from all over the country concerning Bunny. I really believe that it was a miracle that Nancy was able to help me find Bunny.

Note: Interestingly enough, Nancy was not mentioned by name in any of the numerous newspaper articles that appeared about the search for Bunny. In this case, as with all her police work, she stays behind the scenes. Perhaps in the future, when people in general are more open to psychics, there will be more mention of these silent helpers by name.

APPENDIX E
RECOUNTING:
NANCY O'CONNOR SPEAKS

Besides the story of my horse which Nancy has told, I remember a lot about the Thursday night meetings she held in her home. One in particular was very dramatic for me.

For many years I had been in terrible pain with my back. My orthopedist had taken X-rays and did not believe I could get through life without a back operation. He saw a narrowing of the spaces between the vertebrae. The pain had started with my third pregnancy. I had not been able to pick up anything that weighed more than five pounds for several years. I could never lie down on my back or my stomach. The pain was very intense. I did not want a back operation, so I tried to live with it.

We were learning healing techniques in the class one Thursday night, and each member was taking turns sending healing energy to each other. One of us would be the healer, while another was lying on the sofa being the "patient." Many of us remarked at how powerful the atmosphere was.

Unbelievably, the back pain left me after that night. I still was very careful with my back for about a year, not really trusting the fact that the pain had vanished. To this day the pain has never returned. It has never returned, and this healing took place around 1976.

During another meeting Nancy turned off the lights, although some backlighting remained. We were all just sitting there concentrating on Nancy. When it was over, we all reported seeing the same thing. We all saw Nancy's neck elongate and compress, elongate and compress, just like a rubber figure. Her head went up and down and up and down. Afterwards, she told us we were seeing the mental exercises she was doing while she was sitting.

There were many kinds of experiences like that in which it was brought home to us how much power Nancy had and could generate. She was also able to bring this power out in all of us, and we developed our own psychic abilities somewhat. The Thursday night meetings were very, very exciting. They were like our lifeline. Nancy also started a psychic abilities class for children around the same time. My daughters attended these meetings and enjoyed them as well.

※※※ ※※※ ※※※

APPENDIX F
RECOUNTING:
GARY MICCO SPEAKS

The day Rachel was killed, the owner of the gas station said that he, (Michael), walked in that day and asked for his job back. He threw him out. This occurred on the same day, but after he killed her.

I can still see it. As you know, I love investigative work. It's born within me I guess. Resourcefulness is one quality you have to have. Knowing full well we were so close, and knowing that whatever it would take to take it that extra inch, that much closer, whatever that might be, I just knew I had to do that (to meet Nancy). Personally I sensed it. I knew that anyone in law enforcement can't do any job by themselves. You know that when a citizen spots a license plate or a psychic has a vision. I don't care if it's the crazy woman who lives 200 miles away. You know the movie, *Missing Without a Trace*, no one listens to them. Listen to everyone. You have to.

There was a lot going on. That was Thursday night. Friday morning I had been asleep three or four hours, one of the guys on post with me called and told me they found her, "She's dead, get out here right away." I spoke with Nancy once or twice during that period but I don't remember the context of the conversation. Vividly I recall that night, besides the chaos, he (Michael) returned to his home, we had a body Friday night. After we had the body, we went to the house, a bunch of us. He wasn't there. We went to the woods, search party, choppers, everything again. About 20 minutes into it I knew it would be tough. We had people all over the place, volunteers, massive effort.

I returned home finally to sleep, probably for about an hour. Then the phone rings, "Gary, he went to the house, came in, did something, his parents called, cooperating."

He ran out, cross the road. He returned again, I believe, a second time. I'm not sure about this. We're following a nightmare, now it's Saturday. We needed to speak with him. At this point the community, the press, the cameras, the flood of phone calls from the community, all asking what's happening, what's going on. You know, you've got the body, now where's the bad guy. We put together a meeting at West Morris Central High School. We announced it was for the community. It was set for Sunday. I remember going through this. Each day, only getting a few hours of sleep. It was like going to a theater, a horror, but you're one of the actors and you're there every day. Watching this whole thing fall apart, terrible. From an investigator's standpoint, a great experience. Personal standpoint, wish it never happened. Terrible, absolutely terrible. There was a meeting at the High School. I showed up on auto-pilot. You just show up, you know what you have to do. One downfall I have, I just can't shut off. Don't know what to do, go, go, go, go, go. The switch isn't working, just stuck on. Feeling like you're that close, so close, yet not there. Standing there with the Chief of Police and I said "There's a woman who's a psychic, she wants to help and maybe we should listen." The county prosecutor is saying, "You know we can do this ourselves." "We should listen," I repeated and the Chief of Police put his arm around my shoulder and said, "You do what you feel you have to do." I called Nancy in minutes. She needed something that he touched or was with. I brought her a noose, because there was one point in the search of this dump area we found this suicide note and noose. It was like a wire cable of some sort. I got that and brought it to Nancy. I waited for her outside a church in my car at 10:00 PM. I didn't tell her about the note or what the wire was.

After Nancy pulled up in her car, came into mine, talked and broke the ice, I gave her the wire. She said to me "He's heavily drugged with some over the counter pharmaceutical."

Try to find him, that's my purpose for meeting with Nancy. We're trying to find him. Where the hell is he? Nancy said there's grass around him, you can't see him but he can see you. He's on a hill, there is a body of water around or near him, whether it be a puddle or a lake I can't tell. There's also a 50 gallon drum. She then drew a diagram of where the drum was. Some time went by, then Nancy told us he was waiting for his father to come back. She could see his house. She said, "He's going to be caught very soon, he's beginning to come down the hill." Just then the sergeant came on the radio announcing that he (Michael) was in the house"

The next day I took the map with me and figuratively stood on it, by the 50 gallon drum. Looked around and there was everything Nancy laid out on the map she drew exactly as I was seeing it around me.

Rushed to the scene. He was picked up at the house, rushed to the squad room in Long Valley where I jumped in the ambulance and read him his Miranda rights. He was without a doubt out of it. At the hospital they pumped his stomach because he had taken something like Tylenol Cold tablets, a zillion of them. I don't remember. After his stomach was pumped we read him his rights again at the hospital. The first thing in the hospital, it was dark and he looked at me, he was lying in bed, he had a tube down to his stomach still pumping stuff, and he was the 'fraidest thing I ever saw. I said, "It's time to talk about it." He had told me in the ambulance it's time to talk about it. He was sitting up in the hospital bed with a look on his face, and he says, "I was driving down the road and my car broke down and I parked it and I got out to take a leak, I looked down and there she was." He covered his eyes as he said that, as he put his hands on his face he screamed, "There she is, there she is, she's a bloody mess." I interjected quickly, "What did you do?" He continued, "I, I, I, grabbed her, I dragged her, I buried her, sticks, rocks," his voice was frantic, "whatever I could find, I ran, I ran." That was basically as far as we got. Not, "I did it to her," but "I found her, there she is, bloody mess, I'm scared, I don't know what to do."

The following day, Monday, is when he confessed.

GARY CONTINUES - Another story

Let's go on to the next case, the fingerprints, this was the coolest one. There was a burglary of a pharmacy in Long Valley. October 17, 1986, Long Valley Pharmacy, burglary. Respond, port of entry, it's a plaza, it had double doors, and then 15" of window running parallel to these doors, as high as these doors. Bottom part of the left window is broken, smashed. Subject goes in, steals $800 in cash, a couple of thousand pain killers, Dilaudid, Demerol, Percodan, so forth. Walk around the scene, survey the scene, back at the port of entry, pull out the fingerprinting kit, dust for prints, we find an index finger, tip of an index finger, half of the last joint on a piece of broken glass. We lift it, and keep the lift. We look through every known suspect, we're striking out. I go to Nancy and remembering the homicide case I figured she needed something of the guy. I got the guy's fingerprints, this is cool. So I walk in with this file without telling Nancy about it except a basic one liner. I handed her the print and she said she had never held a fingerprint before. She started flipping it around saying this is wild, she's sitting Indian style with her cats, and flipping through this thing. She described a person, she said he was in his twenties, strange looking, pock marked skin, and he had a deformity with his left side of his body. His left arm had a problem. She said we would get him, he's a drug addict, he will do it again and again.

Almost one year later to the day, that fingerprint you had held, we had read a bulletin, Morris County Prosecutor's Office, that a guy was arrested in New Jersey for pharmacy burglaries, ran the print for a match, got a hit. I remember exactly what you had described to me about this person and I was so curious. His father brought him in to be served with the warrants here at headquarters. Showed up, walked through the door and there he was. He was the guy, just as you described, he was 29 years old. In taking the mug shots of him, his arm was wiped out, big time from a propeller and he had taken painkillers that addicted him. He wasn't a criminal before the accident.

I don't know if he came out of the hospital a drug addict. Maybe he did drugs then and left the hospital okay. Maybe he was walking around feeling crappy one day and decided that the drug did make him feel good, let's go back and do that.

I'm not a hard-nosed street cop who has a big male ego who has to do it all himself. I am a resourceful person who will use whatever is given to me, in terms of getting the goal accomplished. Gratefully, I'll add. There are people who help me achieve whatever I have to achieve. From a law enforcement standpoint Nancy is a hell of a tool. I would absolutely recommend using her on a case.

I'm not talking about any psychic, forget about the vision part of it. She's a bright person. She can plug herself into a situation and feel it, be there. When a detective goes to a crime scene he needs to do that at the crime scene, before he pulls his camera out, throws the dust around, forget it. When Nancy goes to a crime scene, when a detective goes to a crime scene and he's looking for the bad guy, he better put all his equipment down, open his eyes, open his ears, walk around the scene. We're trained to look around for evidence, not for the feel of the place.

Nancy's way of seeing has rubbed off on me. Taking the tool that you have, the ability you have. I got a call to a burglary where people were away for a week and got back. A weapon was taken, a lot of jewelry and some money. I showed up at the house at about 3:00 PM. Port of entry was a broken window in the back of the house, entry through the kitchen. Just before they left for vacation they cleaned, vacuumed the rugs, cleaned everything. You don't pick up the camera, you don't pick up the dusting equipment, you sit everyone down. Of course you've got to preserve the scene, the evidential aspect of it. You walk around the house, see what you feel, see what you see, don't just look at it, soak in it, feel it, be the guy. Remember in *Caddyshack*, be the ball man, I remember that. Be the ball, you're walking through the house, and I said to myself yes, you've got one guy here because here we have the port of entry, the kitchen, and we can cut through the dining room to get to the stairs. This guy makes a beeline through the dining area with work boot tracks. Cool, we can follow him, you walk upstairs to the right, the master bedroom is to the left at the end of the house. Look at his stride, he even skipped a couple of stairs, he knew where he was going. Make a right, went into a girl's room. Beds all messed up, drawers pulled out, footprints, footprints, footprints. Forget about fingerprints, who needs them, look at this, he then makes one trip down the hall, stops at a boy's room, picks up some sort of toy, a ball perhaps, then goes to the master bedroom, takes some jewelry, takes a gun. So we see where the stuff is being taken. So I've got the father for twenty minutes. I don't need fingerprints. Let's just look at this, feel it, this guy's got such an interest in the girl's room, you can just walk in his footsteps, because of spending time with Nancy.

Not only what she sees and feels, but her ability to teach someone. Not that I was there to be taught, but as I said unless you listen, you won't hear it, and watch and pick up.

Well, we went to the father. We see a great deal of interest in the girl's room. The father said his daughter is 19. Tell me about your daughter. She's a student, attractive and hands me her picture. She's got several boyfriends. I say, "Name them." This poor man starts pulling names out of a hat. He rolled them out fast, "Billy, Bobby, Tommy, Johnny, Smith, Eddy," "Smith, stop," I said. Smith, why Smith? Something just stood out. "Tell me about Smith. Yeah, tell me about him, what's he drive, etc." Then basic police work kicked in. Go to the neighbor's house. "Seen any vehicle there?"

"Oh yeah, for two days I saw this vehicle." She describes it. Go back to the father. "What does Smith drive?" Describes the same vehicle the neighbor just described. Smith was there for two days, staying at the house. Smith knew they were on vacation. I have the girl call her friend who knows Smith. The friend says, "Yeah, he was target practicing at a quarry in the woods recently, with a 22." It's missing from this house. Picked him up in two hours.

We need all the equipment, we need the stuff we're shown in the Police Academy, I'm impatient, so sometimes my downfall is I don't know when to stop, I should know when, but I don't, I want to get to the end. If you hand me a letter and it has a summary, I'll go to the summary.

Observation and soaking up the scene. It can be taught to others. If I had never met Nancy, it's probably something I might have developed at some point. It also gives you more self-confidence, boosts you a bit. Not to pretend I'm psychic, because I don't think I am or pretend to be when I'm walking around the house, but to walk through and observe and soak it in at work, before you even begin to pick up the equipment you were taught to use, you better know how to use that part of you.

WASHINGTON TOWNSHIP
POLICE DEPARTMENT
LONG VALLEY, MORRIS COUNTY, NEW JERSEY

908-876-3232
FAX 908-876-5655

P.O. BOX 421
LONG VALLEY, N.J. 07853-0421

GEORGE W. KLUETZ
CHIEF

March 1, 1995

To Whom It May Concern:

     I have had occasion to call upon the services of Nancy Weber for criminal investigations. I have found her services to be useful and her direction to be reliable.

Sincerely,

[signature]

Ptl. Gary Micco
Wash. Twp. P.D.
(Morris County)

GM:bd

LETTER FROM GARY MICCO

APPENDIX G
RECOUNTING:
BILL HUGHES SPEAKS

I went from a non believer to a believer in one day. I was awestruck by this case.

The first experience I had with Nancy was the arson of the White Brothers Tire Company. I was a new detective at the time. I was working with another detective named Eddie, and we went out for a ride with her. We went to the place and drove around it for a short period of time. She had the feeling the arson was caused by a vagrant or a passerby. We never really did track down who had done it, but what struck me as funny on that particular day was that I was riding in the back seat and she was in the front seat. There was dead silence in the car for two or three minutes. Suddenly she looked over at Eddie, smiled and said, "You will never know." It had nothing to do with the crime. Eddie looked shocked. Later at the station, he confided in me that he had some embarassing thoughts on his mind. He was as white as a ghost. This incident was funny, but it was eye-opening for me. I said to myself, "I've got to be careful what I think around this woman!"

In the Koedatich case, Tim was the captain in Parsippany at the time, the head of the detective bureau. He was heading the investigation at the time from the Parsippany end of it. Nancy made him a believer and things took off from there. He had very high feelings and praise for what she did on that case. The main problem with working with psychics is selling the boss on the issue, especially if he has never had any experience in this area. Really, though, we used Nancy more or less on our own. I don't think it was sanctioned by anybody. There were several things that came out before an arrest was made. I recall her describing Koedatich to a tee. She had his height, his build, and said he was of Czech or Polish descent. She went on to say that he had served time in prison before and that he had killed before. All these things turned out to be true. After Deidre O'Brien had been kidnapped and killed we went out driving. We went up to the rest area where she was murdered. We drove through there, we got off at exit 19, and got back on Interstate 80 going eastbound. Nancy said that was the route Koedatich had taken. She told me to get off at the Wharton exit because he had connections in Wharton. We later found out that he worked there. He was a superintendent of an apartment complex there. This took place all on one day.

A few days later we went out driving again. Something kept coming into her head. It was the name of the park, Louis Morris park. It was on Route 24 right across the street from where Deirdre was kidnapped. She couldn't understand why the name Louis Morris kept coming into your head. At that time she didn't know where she was kidnapped from. When we took her to the scene it all came together. I guess he must have spent some time with her in Louis Morris Park before he took her up to the rest area on the highway.

Nancy saw an American flag in a vision, but it turned out to be American Road down in Morris Plains. And a woman's shoe was on the street. Nothing was ever found out about this. No one was ever reported missing. We think it may have been a domestic violence situation which neither party ever reported.

The Mendham Township Police didn't follow up on any of the leads Nancy gave — Coleman, the three motor vehicle violation tickets. Probably because they were skeptical. When Koedatich was stopped for the motor violations it was just a chance stop, so they didn't bother looking through the car. It's very sad. They did find the evidence in the end, the same evidence which Nancy saw.

Working with a psychic was fascinating, utterly fascinating. I went in with an open mind. You need to have an open mind in this world where so many things are incomprehensible. It didn't take long to convince me though. I was just in awe through every minute of it. Any time I could get together with her I was all for it. I recall I did a lot of it on my own time. I wasn't getting paid overtime or anything. Even though we were working under tragic circumstances I enjoyed it. My feelings, and I'm sure Nancy's, were with the families, but the opportunity to work with her was fascinating to me.

I would say that there are probably a lot of people, not just officers, who have the ability but don't realize it. They may visualize something happening, but when it happens they just shrug it off as a coincidence. I would say officers could probably be trained. I think law enforcement ought to utilize this. There are so many cases that run into dead ends but they are not dead cases. Law enforcement is just too skeptical to utilize something like that. As I see it for myself, I wouldn't use it on a real strong case. Something that was cut and dried. If I had a case with no leads, or with too many leads and I had to weed them out it could come in handy. You don't want to be spending weeks chasing useless leads when your good leads are going cold on you. The longer it takes to solve a case, the harder it is.

I don't feel a psychic should be asked to work for nothing. Even though governments use psychics they do not admit it, and they are not prepared to make those kind of expenditures. They are afraid they could not justify them to the public. We were very fortunate to have had Nancy donate her time to help us. They never would have paid for her though.

Funds are not available for experimental testing, however they could be made available for training. That could possibly be appropriated. But so many people want the hard, cold facts. They need proof that it works first.

I see that there is more to the universe than we know. It's one thing to think these things, but another to experience them.

When I was in school my favorite subject was science. A lot of science deals in the realm of positives. Something is or it isn't. But Nancy opened up the gray area, telling me that anything in this universe is possible. There are a lot of people out there who say they're psychic, but they have to prove it to me. When I walked into the room Nancy was in, believe me I felt it. She has a strong aura about her. I'm a trusting soul, but sometimes in the back of my mind I might feel a guy is feeding me a line or something. But that's notthat way with Nancy.

APPENDIX H
RECOUNTING:
CAPTAIN DAVID HEATER SPEAKS

The first one we worked on was the still unsolved Princess Doe case. We were introduced by Michele Bochenek. The case that I remember most clearly though is the Elizabeth Cornish case (Elizabeth [Betty] Kramer's married name had been Cornish).

She had been killed with a hammer by John Reese. I remember Nancy came with us to the field where we thought he had tossed the weapon. She described a body of water she was seeing where he had thrown it. Later on we found the spot where we think he threw it. It was a wooded area surrounding a swamp like area that was very deep. Unfortunately we never found the weapon. We did recover a hammer with human blood on it, but it couldn't have made Betty's wounds. It was the wrong shape. The angle was too steep.

Betty's cousin had come to us at first. She had been talking to a psychic, a friend of hers. This always scares me because we get all these supposed psychics calling us. The cousin went on and on. I asked her where this psychic lived and she told me she lived in Flanders. I asked if she was Nancy Fuchs and she said that was who it was. I said, "O.K. Now I'll listen."

The first time I worked with a psychic was in 1972. I don't remember who it was. We had a murder and one of the state police detectives who was very hard-nosed took me for a ride to see this woman. I was skeptical. She had no idea we were coming, and when we arrived she told us how she had solved a murder in Connecticut. She found the body in a drum. She managed to pick out the right drum out of about five hundred of them. I thought it was just a lucky guess. We showed her pictures of our possible suspects. Out of eighteen pictures she picked out the one we suspected the most. She said he was very connected to the murder victim. They knew each other. We found out later that they had been having an affair. We actually think that it was a blackmail type of thing. They had broken up and she was still married. He got into her van with her and I think she jumped out of the van. I don't think she was shoved out of the van as was thought.

I still thought this woman was making another lucky guess. She was looking at the guy's picture and told us there was something wrong with his stomach. We had put him on the polygraph three times, and every time we did his ulcer acted up and we couldn't test him. Then she started talking about seeing a camper driving down Route 57, making a left, there's a big building, a little pond. I started to think about what she was talking about. There was a twenty-five minute block of time we were missing here, so I figured out now that she was taking us up to a place called Ingersoll Dam, which is an out of the way lovers' area type of thing. After speaking to her we go back and clock the drive, and it's exactly twenty-five minutes from the way she took us up the mountain. The way they probably came back they ended up on the road where she jumped out. After that I was convinced that there are people who can actually see things. Then after that when I spoke with Nancy on the Princess Doe case, that sealed my confidence.

I went through police academy training when I received my badge. It was so obvious that psychology was lacking in the training. It's scary. Sometimes a cop turns out to be a bad guy. Perhaps they should have been psychologically tested in the beginning. Training as a psychic, also, is not so far afield from the study of psychology. You can certainly show people ways to get into their own subconscious.

Betty's father was very upset, yet he was much more together. He was doing everything he could to help. Betty's daughter was a real problem at the time because she didn't want to talk to us either. She was fourteen or fifteen at the time. It turned out, really, that Betty was an alcoholic. We didn't care about that, but we did want to know what her habits were, where she went, was she drunk the night of the murder, maybe unconscious, etc. We just wanted to catch the bad guy.

The chief suspect at the time was Betty's boyfriend. He said he had not been to her house the night of the murder, but he was supposed to have gone. He decided to show up later and found her dead. We suspected him because he would not talk to us.

I sat by the bed and I remember Nancy sat by me and said she was seeing a red haired bearded guy with a scar on his cheek and a Western belt buckle.

I realized it sounded like she was describing the same man in the Princess Doe case. She was describing John Reese, Betty's upstairs neighbor. I didn't remember the scar on the cheek though, and decided to look into it. We started looking into him. We brought him in for fingerprints. We had a fingerprint from Betty's window. We had brought in a window pane and compared them. We kept picking Reese up to talk to him because the guy I was working with had a bad feeling about the story he was giving. It just rubbed him the wrong way for whatever reason. As we kept going over Reese's story with him, we found more and more inconsistencies. We found out many things were not true. We even polygraphed him. He passed, and we eliminated him as a suspect for a while. I still felt there was something wrong about this guy. We were going on our intuition. After all this was over and he was convicted, we realized he was only giving us the story until about 2:30 in the morning the night the homicide occurred. When we polygraphed him we realized we didn't take him far enough into the early morning, and he wasn't lying about the events up until that time. If we had taken him beyond 2:30 AM we would have gotten him right away.

There was a juried trial. We had a video taped confession that describes to some degree what I believe occurred. We know through blood stain interpretation that there were three different areas of attack in Betty's apartment. He claims she let him in at the door, but based on the bloodstain patterns he got in either through the window or the door and hit her on the head with the hammer as she was sleeping.

I trusted Nancy, having worked with her on Princess Doe. Every time you have a murder case you get all kinds of people calling up saying they are psychic. I don't know if they're having dreams or whatever, but once you start talking to them you realize that nothing is clicking or making any sense at all. The things that Nancy came out with were eventually found to be true.

I heard from Michele Bohenek that Reese is on the video of both Betty's and Princess Doe's funeral. I know he attended Betty's. Nancy feels he may have killed both of them. She believes he met Princess Doe and was with her in the pizza parlor.

When we went back to the pizza place during the Princess Doe investigation, Nancy pointed out that it is across from the cemetery. We hypnotized a lady who came out with a perfect description of the dress. She sees her talking to a guy in the A&P right in the town of Blairstown. She gave us a partial description and the guy had a beard. One interesting thing about Reese we found after interviewing his past girlfriends is that one of them said that she literally escaped from him with her life. He was chasing her with a knife through a corn field. Her father lived on the other side of the field. She had a seventy-five to a hundred yard run and outran him to the house.

Nancy had told me that the one who killed Princess Doe was a serial killer. Reese was so cool during his confession. Absolutely no remorse. None during the whole trial.

When Nancy spoke to me early on, I was very fixed on Betty Kramer's boyfriend as the murderer. That was because he wouldn't talk to us. I think now that he was a bit in shock. He talked about being a fisherman and there were a set of clippers found outside at the back end of Betty's apartment. If the killer went in through the window above he might have dropped them trying to scramble into that window. They had a little string on them sort of like a fisherman would use. We kept trying to get him to explain why these clippers were there. Also, he wasn't showing a lot of remorse either. This really rubbed me the wrong way. I thought he was being too cool. We wanted him to submit to blood samples and a polygraph test but he wouldn't until he spoke to his attorney. I thought if he didn't do it, what was the big deal?

After Reese had passed the polygraph I was sort of fixed on the fact that Reese had nothing to do with it until Nancy mentioned him. I was still trying to work on eliminating the boyfriend and getting him to talk. His attorney was stonewalling me, and my partner was coming at me with different things. It finally got to the point where the last night that we had Reese he told Gary that he was out drinking and returned home while his girlfriend was working a double shift. There was a big block of time we couldn't account for. He said he was out on the stoop drinking a beer. The other thing that we had was that Reese told us about another guy sitting on another stoop across the quad who saw him drinking. You had told me about a guy on a stoop and I wondered whether it was Reese himself or the other guy you had been seeing. Gary asked Reese at that point, where he was during the missing block of time between twelve thirty and two o'clock in the morning. The more Reese kept talking the more inconsistencies he had. Gary, and two other guys, Tommy and Pat and I sat there and went over Reese's whole story. You could see in Reese's face that he wasn't telling us everything. This was the first time he spoke about sitting on the stoop having a beer. You talked about some guy sitting on the stoop having a beer and being the killer, so now I'm eliminating this guy across the courtyard. Now, my fixation with the boyfriend is over too. So Pat jumped up and said, "I know you did it, and you know you did it. Why don't you just tell us?" Reese clammed up and went into a fixed stare. Pat walked over to him, sat down and started talking to him like a Dutch Uncle. He said, "Look, the worst of this is over. We know you did it. You might as well tell us what happened." Gary and Tommy left the room at that point and left us alone with Reese. Reese got to the point where he said he wanted to talk to an attorney before he told us what happened. We called the other two guys back in to watch him, but not to speak to him until he reached his attorney. Pat and I went to talk to the prosecutor about what we had gotten on Reese so far. We heard conversation going on in the room where we had left Reese. We went back in and told them to knock it off. Reese said, "Wait a minute, I want to talk to these guys. I know I asked for an attorney, I don't want to see one now, I just want to talk to these guys." The prosecutor went in, and when he heard him say he did not want the attorney he said to go ahead and talk. That is when he confessed. We videotaped him as he went through the whole story.

I think he confessed because we had enough inconsistencies on him. I also think it was when Pat said, "We know you did it." And I think he was relieved.

People like Reese seem to say, "Stop me, put me away, I can't stop what I'm doing. You have to stop me." Yeah, you know he really didn't fight us. We had let him walk away with his girlfriend in the courtyard that night. I think it was getting to the point where he knew we had him cornered, and he could have run but didn't.

His girlfriend was working a double shift and he was telling us how great their sex life was and that he had such a tremendous sex drive. He basically wanted to get laid and that's all there was to it. He knew that Betty was supposed to be a "hot number" downstairs. This was really a sexually motivated murder.

According to our investigation, Diane Dye (whom we believe to be Princess Doe) out in California is missing to this day. We interviewed twenty or thirty guys out there who had sexual relations with her when she was thirteen or fourteen years old. She probably got across the country as a hooker. The San Jose police department had never been able to locate her since the day she left her door. We placed her in Daly City about six months before the murder of Princess Doe occurred. We have people verifying the fact that she was there, which is the westernmost portion of Route 80. She probably hitchhiked across country with truck drivers and ended up on this end of Route 80. (Blairstown). Then somehow she ended up with Reese, we think.

I'm not sure what he was doing back in 1982. He was living in the area in Columbia, New Jersey. That's right next to Route 80. When we locked him up he was working on a sod farm operating heavy machinery.

AFTERWORD:
AUTHORS' COMMENTS

IRIS SPEAKS:

I first met Nancy Weber in the fall of 1987. She had no advance information about me, and in fact only knew my first name. She held my hands for a few seconds, became very calm, and quietly said, "I see books all around you." There was no way, except by psychically "reading me," that she could have known that books were a very large, very important part of my life.

As a withdrawn child, my nose was always buried in a book. This started with large picture books before I could actually read, and later extended into the printed word. As a teenager I began to collect out of print illustrated children's' books...many of them my old childhood friends. This led into a part time occupation of purchasing these books and re-selling them to other collectors.

Eventually, a friend got me intrigued with the marbleized end papers found in many early books, and I soon after fell into my current occupation of paper marbling. These papers, nowadays, are used for book binding and restoration.

I have written four technical manuals on the Art of marbling: *Traditional Marbling; Fabric Marbling; 105 Helpful Marbling Hints;* and *Varieties of Spanish Marbling.* I have also re-issued a facsimile reprint of *A Manual Of The Art Of Bookbinding,* which was the first American manual on bookbinding by James B. Nicholson (1856). It had a section on marbling with original specimens of marbled paper that were also hand marbled for the reprint.

My most interesting book story concerns the writing of *Varieties of Spanish Marbling,* which had been handed to me in a dream by a colleague who had died the previous year.

During our first meeting Nancy also told me I had been a marbler in two previous lives. She proceeded to give me a completely accurate history of marbling, with a few additions, which were later discovered to be true when new information on marbling came to the attention of historians. I was also given a family name from one of these lives, the name belonged to a family of French nobility in the 1500's. I later discovered that this particular family was embroiled in an ongoing feud with another noble family from Germany during this time period. Ironically, I am now a descendant of this same German family according to a relative. Neither Nancy or I knew this at the time.

Nancy Orlen Weber (a modern day Maid of Orleans?........Orlen was originally Orleans when her grandparents came from France and Latvia), was born on February 11, 1944 in Brooklyn, New York. She is a registered nurse, psychic, healer, counselor, clergy person, artist, poet, police investigator, wife, mother, songwriter and dancer. She has had, and continues to lead a very full life, full of unusual and exciting experiences. Yet she is, in most ways an ordinary person and shares the same joys and sorrows as the rest of us. What is different about her is her extrasensory ability to see and hear the things that are all around us, but most people have tuned out.

What made her this way? Certainly some people are more "open" to these other levels than most, but in many cases psychics have had either traumatic or at least very difficult early years. These difficulties have often forced them to turn inward, and perhaps listen to the voice within. This is certainly true in Nancy's case, which we have seen in the chapters where she speaks of her life.

Nancy's story is somewhat different from most biographies of psychics, as the main focus is not entirely on the amazing feats she has performed. These are of course told, but more importantly, the message behind these events is stressed. Such messages as the synchronicity and connectedness of all life; the trauma of early childhood abuse, and how we must all become aware of this horrible tragic problem and do what we can to put an end to it; how we can all tap into our immense potential for creativity in every form; and how we can all be released from the self imprisonment of chaos and confusion in our lives by starting to really see. Nancy's life is a model for all these ideals, and it is hoped that the ideas in this book will help others see the world in a different way.

I wondered whether I was the right person to write this book with her, as all my previous writing work had been technical publications. Nancy felt the coincidence of our two dreams (see prologue) and the prediction of the other psychic was too much to ignore. We had a discussion about this, and I was still feeling a bit uncertain, when another signpost appeared...a book fell off my book shelf in the middle of the night. When I looked to see what it was I was astounded...it was a biography on the life of Sylvia Brown, another well-recognized psychic. Whether this has any significance or was just a strange coincidence, we cannot be sure.

NANCY SPEAKS:

The synchronicity of the wheel of action and response (karma) is awesome. The wheel seems to spin tighter with increased meditation, discipline of mind and time. I have come to believe the murderers, rapists and others who commit heinous crimes, besides having come from trauma at some point, reach out to grab another soul to hold onto who will never forget them, even after death. The criminals perhaps are even more terrified than the victim, for they cannot afford to feel truly alone in their own soul. They cling to anger, hate and destruction to avoid the agony of their true belief, that they have been completely and totally rejected long before their first crime. It is their early role model of rejection as a way of being remembered that they perpetuate. Let us not for a moment believe that this understanding of what motivates is intended to lessen the remedial action needed to create change. We need to move beyond our fear and frustration into purposeful and creative legislation, lobbying and greater concern for all who come to this earth.

On a personal note, I communicate with the victims who have left this earth, pray with them for peace and seek to create change here so that others may not suffer at the hands of the most frightened element of our species. In seeking the murderers, rapists and other violent-minded people, I seek to communicate with their souls and encourage an alternate path, where they can release their need to exploit others.

Currently a group of friends have worked with me to develop a project for pre-natal stress management. We hope to help create a better start in life for all. It is my dream and belief that our world would be a more loving place if all children were born into kinder environments.

For missing children, Dick and I created a concept that would enable children of about two years of age and up to call for help without having to say anything. Michele Bochenek and another friend, Howard Steinberg, are developing the project with us and we are currently discussing the idea with a major corporation.

Out of the fire of destruction, an honoring of a purpose produces a possibility of change amongst all of us. I only hope that some of these ideas that have floated to my consciousness are seeds that bear good and healthy fruit.

To be added to Nancy's mailing list, or for information on lectures, workshops and sessions please send a #10 SASE to:

The Unlimited Mind
P.O. Box 1132
Denville, New Jersey 07834

Tapes by Nancy

The World Within - Nancy's voice will guide you through a beautiful fantasy to the accompaniment of stress free music.

Light Passages - Mother-to-be and baby will begin the bonding process in this magical visualization. Can be used in delivery room. A manual is included.

Awakening - You will quickly discover your creative potential as you begin to use and balance both hemispheres of the brain.

Nurturing - Your eating habits can be changed as a lovingly, healthier outlook on your body needs, begins to take form.

Order Form

Name_____

Address_____

_____

_____

Make Checks payable to:
The Unlimited Mind
Box 1132
Denville, NJ 07834

The World Within _____tapes @ $10.00 _____

*Light Passages with manual*_____tapes @ $15.50 _____

*Awakening*_____tapes @ $10.00_____

Nurturing _____tapes @ $10.00_____

Shipping & Handling $3.00 for first item/ea.add.l add $1 _____

New Jersey Residents add 6% sales tax _____

Total enclosed $_____